Sermons
ON
THE
Couch

Sermons

ON THE Couch

A YEAR OF
INSPIRATIONAL REFLECTIONS

CINDY GENTRY

HAY HOUSE, INC.
Carlsbad, California • New York City
London • Sydney • New Delhi

Published in the United States by: Hay House, Inc.: www.hayhouse .com® • *Published in Australia by:* Hay House Australia Pty. Ltd.: www .hayhouse.com.au • *Published in the United Kingdom by:* Hay House UK, Ltd.: www.hayhouse.co.uk • *Published in India by:* Hay House Publishers India: www.hayhouse.co.in

Cover design: Micah Kandros
Interior design: Karim J. Garcia

**Cataloging-in-Publication Data is on file
at the Library of Congress**

Tradepaper ISBN: 978-1-4019-7264-6
E-book ISBN: 978-1-4019-7265-3
Audiobook ISBN: 978-1-4019-7266-0

10 9 8 7 6 5 4 3 2 1
1st edition, July 2023

Printed in the United States of America

For my dad—
who left poverty and prejudice behind him and raised me to
be a strong, independent woman. Somewhere somehow, I know
you're seeing this all unfold and cheering me on. I'll meet you on
the other side.

CONTENTS

Part 3: Wonders

Part 4: Gifts

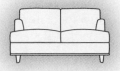

WELCOME!

A few years ago, I had the great and good fortune to join a Facebook group set up by who else? Facebook God. It was filled with funny posts and heartwarming stories of loved ones who had crossed over into the Great Beyond. When trolls invaded the space, Facebook God created a private group called Heaven.

All was good there for a while, too, until people started bickering over things like whether one should be a vegan, vegetarian, or meat-eater. For some reason, this inspired me to create my first "Sermon on the Couch," a tongue-in-cheek take on the Sermon on the Mount. People then requested weekly sermons and so here we are—from post, to blog, to this book.

From time to time, we all need an inspiring word, or something to make us laugh, or a good song to crank up and lift our mood. So, grab your favorite beverage and curl up and get cozy as we carve out some space for reflection together in these hectic and often unsettling times. I hope these sermons will help create a calming space for you— whether you read them weekly, when the mood strikes, or whether you choose to seek out ones that speak to a specific situation in your life.

In writing these sermons, I've been mindful that religion has had a positive impact on some and a negative impact on others. For me, it's been rather a mixed bag. So, wherever you find yourself on the religious and spiritual spectrums—or any other spectrum—know that you have a place here.

For each sermon, you'll find a "hymn" or two. My taste in music is nothing if not eclectic so there's everything from oldies but goodies to some modern gems. I've included the artists and song titles, and you can also access the entire playlist on Spotify or YouTube by searching for "Sermons on the Couch ~ Hymns."

You'll also find a section at the end of each sermon for reflection (if you'd like) with guiding questions. Feel free to write, sketch, or doodle whatever thoughts you'd like to capture.

So, Dearest, let us go forth in peace and gratitude and may the Universe shower us with blessings.

Amen.

Part 1: Miracles

LIFE IS A SERIES OF THOUSANDS OF TINY MIRACLES. NOTICE THEM.

— Anonymous

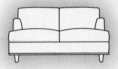

RESOLUTIONS

Hello, most precious and powerful Angels. Gather close as we figuratively join hands and join hearts to come together for a little while of quiet reflection.

It's that time of year when everyone's talking about resolutions. For many of us, the past year was amazing, while for others the year is best relegated to the dumpster, doused with an accelerant of choice, and burned into oblivion. In either case, we look to the start of this year as a time of new beginnings.

So, we make resolutions. And while it's important to strive for improvement, all too often, we end up feeling guilt or shame when we don't follow through. Ain't nobody got time for that. Instead, I propose we set some modest intentions—for ourselves, our loved ones, and our world.

What can you do for yourself, Dearest, to be a happier, healthier person? You must start by putting that oxygen mask on first. It can be as simple as going for a walk, staying hydrated, or throwing a few more veggies on your plate. If you're ready for more of a challenge, stop putting off going to the doctor, letting that gym membership lie fallow, or waiting to sign up for that 5K. And for those Angels up for the master class challenge—dust off that dream. As wise person Jean Shinoda Bolen said, "When you recover or discover something that nourishes your soul and brings you joy, care enough about yourself to make room for it in your life." Write that book, take that class, go to that audition, start that business.

What can you do to improve your relationship with your loved ones? For some of us, it means taking steps to remove them if they are toxic. As wise person Steven Bartlett said, "You don't lose real friends, real opportunities, or real relationships when you start standing up for yourself and setting clear boundaries. You lose abusers, manipulators, narcissists, control freaks, attention seekers, and mental-health-destroying leeches."

For some, it means prioritizing spending time together or working on our own issues to be more present for those we value. Wise person Dean Koontz said, "That anger harms no one more than he who harbors it. That both bitterness and true happiness are choices we make, not conditions that fall upon us from the hands of fate. That peace is to be found in the acceptance of things we are unable to change. That friends and family are the blood of life, and that the purpose of existence is caring, commitment."

And what can we do to make the world a better place? We can start by sprucing up our little corner of it. Can you pick up trash at the beach? Plant a little neglected patch of dirt? Write letters to seniors or those recovering from cancer? Pay the toll or buy the coffee of the person behind you? As wise person Scott Adams said, "Remember, there is no such thing as a small act of kindness. Every act creates a ripple with no logical end."

Until next time, may we go in peace and gratitude, may this shiny new year bring us our heart's desires, and may the Universe shower us with blessings.

Amen.

Our hymn for today is *New Beginning* by Tracy Chapman. Let us sing.

Take a moment to reflect on your past experiences with creating resolutions. What might you do differently this year?

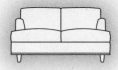

FLAWS

Hello again, most dear and darling Angels. Gather close as we again figuratively join hands and join hearts to come together for a little while of quiet reflection.

I come to you today to talk about our flaws—both real and perceived. Many of us spend so much time feeling guilt and shame over them. But, Dearest, you are perfect in your imperfection. As wise person Marc Hack said, "Let someone love you just the way you are—as flawed as you might be, as unattractive as you sometimes feel, as unaccomplished as you think you are. To believe that you must hide all the parts of you that are broken, out of fear that someone is incapable of loving what is less than perfect, is to believe that sunlight is incapable of entering through a broken window and illuminating a dark room."

Some of you may be familiar with the Japanese art of kintsugi, where artisans take shattered bowls, vases, and the like and repair the cracks with silver or gold. The idea is that the piece is more beautiful for having been broken. It is also infinitely more valuable for the precious metal holding it together—just as we are for having survived what was meant to destroy us.

Many of the people that contributed to our world were ordinary, flawed human beings in extraordinary circumstances. Winston Churchill was arguably the right Prime Minister at the right time, yet he diverted food away from India to Europe, worsening the famine there. Mother Teresa helped the poor and the sick, yet many of her ideas and methods have come into question. So, don't let your fallibility stand in the way of you making a difference. As wise person Alysia Reiner said, "The more I am able to deeply love and accept my flaws and imperfections, the more I am able to do that with my fellows."

I believe you are on this planet at this time for a reason, and clearly, it's all hands on deck. I commend us all to look around—where can we lend a hand, donate, comfort, share? Whether it is at work, in our communities, or on an even larger scale, your unique talents and beautiful heart are needed. It is that very humanness that makes your contribution all the more valuable.

Let us go into the week to come with this wisdom from Stephen Hawking: "One of the basic rules of the Universe is that nothing is perfect. Perfection simply doesn't exist . . . without imperfection, neither you nor I would exist."

As always, may we go in peace and gratitude, may we be patient with ourselves and others, as we are all works in progress, and may the Universe shower us with blessings.

Amen.

In honor of a great and imperfect person, Dr. Martin Luther King, Jr., our hymn for today is *Pride (In the Name of Love)* by U2.

W hat is one flaw that you have struggled with? Could this flaw be something that makes you part of the human family, or is it something you would rather work on?

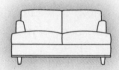

SECOND CHANCES

Hello again, most bright and beautiful Angels. Gather close as we figuratively join hands and join hearts to come together for a little while of quiet reflection.

I come to you today to talk about second chances—for ourselves and perhaps, upon careful consideration, for others. As wise person Holly Elissa Bruno said, "Sure, life as we know it is enough. But life as we don't know it? That's where the magic awaits. That's where second chances abound." Time to take a step of faith into the unknown.

Now, maybe you don't think of yourself as an Angel. Well, I consider anyone reading this to be an Angel, as I've said before—perfect in your imperfections. Let's face it—we've all screwed up. Maybe it was something small, or maybe we messed up in epic proportion. It's what comes after the screwup that determines whether we will grow from the experience or remain stunted.

There are two ways you can ensure that you avoid growth. You can either turn the situation around and blame others for your mistake, or you can bury yourself in regret and condemnation. As wise person Dale Carnegie said, "Any fool can criticize, condemn, and complain—and most fools do."

If you choose to take the path of growth, then the first thing to do is to admit you were wrong—to yourself and to those you have harmed. Offer up a true apology—none of this "my bad" nonsense, or "I'm sorry that you felt bad when I justifiably acted like an ass." Step up, look them in the eye, and say the words, "I'm sorry. I was wrong."

Next, you must make amends. For those of you familiar with 12-step programs, they advise making amends directly to the person or persons unless that would cause them injury. This is about making them feel better, Dearest, not you. If the person has died or it isn't possible for some other reason, then you can always write a letter or say what you would have said to them if you could. As wise person Dale E. Turner said, "It is the highest form of self-respect to admit our errors and mistakes and make amends for them. To make a mistake is only an error in judgment, but to adhere to it when it is discovered shows infirmity of character."

What comes next may be the hardest step of all—forgive yourself. You are worthy of forgiveness. You are not your mistakes. You are a blessed child of the Universe. Lather, rinse, and repeat this as often as necessary until it drowns out any and all negative lies. Today is your day to begin again, sweet Angel. A wise anonymous person said it best: "Whatever you've done before, accept it and let it go. You are not perfect. You are capable of making mistakes. Stop hiding from the shadows of the past. Don't be trapped in the darkness of shattered memories. Let the light pass through and shine on you. Forgive yourself because it's the only way to start again."

Now before I talk about cutting others some slack, a warning. Proceed with caution. There is a fine line between forgiving someone and becoming a doormat.

Wise anonymous people have said, "Sometimes good-bye is a second chance," or "Giving someone a second chance is like providing someone with another bullet after they missed shooting you the first time." Sometimes we are in love with who the person could be rather than the reality of who they are. But if the person has asked for forgiveness, made amends, learned from their mistake, and perhaps most importantly, earned back trust, then it may be at least worth considering a second chance. But as wise person Selena Gomez said, "I believe in second chances, but I don't believe in third or fourth chances."

As always, may we go in peace and gratitude, may each new day be a fresh, clean start, and may the Universe shower us with blessings.

Amen.

Today's hymn is *Try Everything* by Shakira. Let us sing it loud and proud.

> I s there something that you need to forgive yourself for? What would you need to do to make amends for your mistake? Is there someone else in your life who would like a second chance? What steps would he or she need to take to earn back your trust?

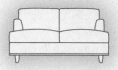

HOPE?

Hello again, most inspiring and incredible Angels. Gather close as we figuratively join hands and join hearts to come together for a little while of quiet reflection.

I come to you today to talk about balancing hope and anxiety. There are times when there is more than enough angst to go around. We find ourselves on a roller-coaster ride of emotion. One minute we are hopefully optimistic, the next woefully pessimistic.

I got to thinking about how, whenever the stakes are high—the beginning of a relationship, waiting to hear about the outcome of an application, lab test, or interview—many of us waiver back and forth on the emotional spectrum. It can be exhausting. So, can we give our weary hearts a place to rest in one spot or the other? Should we? I wish I had a definitive answer. I can't honestly say that I do. But I think there may be some ways to make the waiting time a little more bearable.

A big part of our pessimism is probably due to our fear that we can't handle the outcome of the situation, that it will debilitate us to the point of no return. But, Dearest, that simply isn't true. You've overcome heartbreak that brought you to your knees. You've survived 100 percent of your worst days so far. As wise person Maya Angelou said, "Stand up straight and realize who you are, that you tower over your circumstances."

Once we've put on our game face, it's time to take care of business. Get some clarity on what we can and can't control in the situation. Then put our full effort into the process. We can't make someone love us, but we can put time and effort into ourselves and the relationship. We can't control the hiring decision, but we can try to make a good impression during the interview.

Next, and this is a biggie, we have to let it go. Realizing that the situation is out of our hands is both freeing and frightening as hell. As wise person Melody Beattie said, "Let go of your expectations. The universe will do what it will. Sometimes your dreams will come true. Sometimes they won't. Sometimes when you let go of a broken dream, another one gently takes its place. Be aware of what is, not what you would like to be taking place." Repeat step one—you've got this.

Finally, as always, take care of yourself during these craziest of times. Eat fresh food, hydrate, get some sleep, go outside, do something silly and fun. Take a break from social media. Remind yourself that this is one part of your life—not the only part. There is still so much in this world that is wonderful—our family, our friends, music, coffee, the ocean, laughter. Take a few deep breaths and focus on things that make you happy rather than the gnawing anxiety of waiting to know what comes next.

I think we have to take the necessary steps to protect our tender hearts and our peace of mind. But ultimately, I think we have to err on the side of positivity—otherwise, why are we here? What a sad place a world without hope would be. May these wise words from Winston Churchill inspire us: "I have no fear of the future. Let us go forward into its mysteries, let us tear aside the veils which hide it from our eyes, and let us move onward with confidence and courage."

As always, may we go in peace and gratitude, may we remember how brave we truly are, and may the Universe shower us with blessings.

Amen.

Our hymn for today is *Believe* by Shawn Mendes.
Let us sing.

Think of a situation you are dealing with today. List the things that are and are not in your control. What do you feel ready to let go of this week?

LOVE LANGUAGES

Hello again, most fierce and fabulous Angels. Gather close as we figuratively join hands and join hearts to come together for a little while of quiet reflection.

I come to you today to talk about love and all the ways we express it. Now, I'm certainly no expert in the "pompatus of love," as wise person Steve Miller would say, but several years ago, I had the opportunity to learn about the Five Love Languages in the context of building assets in children. For some reason, they keep coming up this week so it must be time for them to appear in a sermon.

Developed some 25 years ago by Dr. Gary Chapman, the basic premise is that everyone—couples, children, friends, and co-workers—give and receive love in different ways. By discovering the love language that the people in our lives speak, we can improve our relationships and fulfill our needs as well. As wise person Tony Gaskins said, "Love a person the way they need to be loved, not the way you want to love. It's not about you. Love is selfless, not selfish."

So in no particular order . . .

- Words of Affirmation: Folks who respond to this love language appreciate hearing: "I love you"; "I'm proud of you"; "You mean the world to me." You can say it out loud, tuck surprise notes somewhere, or send a text. As wise one Orlando Aloysius Battista said, "The greatest weakness of most humans is their hesitancy to tell others how they love them while they're alive."

- Quality Time: These folks feel loved and appreciated when you dedicate one-on-one time to them. It could be as simple as cooking a meal together, a date night, or taking a walk. We are all busy these days, but as a wise anonymous person advises, "Save the excuses. It's not about 'having' time. It's about making time. If it matters, you will make the time."

- Physical Touch: These people feel loved when you hold hands, kiss them, or snuggle close. As wise person Randi G. Fine said, "No other form of communication is as universally understood as touch. The compassionate touch of a hand or a reassuring hug can take away our fears, soothe our anxieties, and fill the emptiness of being lonely."

- Acts of Service: These folks feel loved when you go out of your way to do something special for them, like filling up their car with gas or helping with a task. As wise one Steve Maraboli said, "A kind gesture can reach a wound that only compassion can heal."

- Giving Gifts: These folks appreciate the thought, not necessarily the expense, and definitely those happy day surprises that are given for no particular reason. As wise person Tinku Razoria said, "Some gifts are big. Some gifts are small. But the ones that come from the heart are the best gifts of all."

I share these, Dearest, for a few reasons. Mostly, it's because I think that a lot of fine people with the best of intentions are either missing it when it comes to showing the important people in their lives that they care, while others are feeling disappointed and misunderstood because they're not receiving the love people are sending. So, if you have a difficult kiddo in your life or you feel like a relationship is not where you'd like it to be, consider these ideas. And, as a matter of self-care, find out what your needs are and communicate them to your loved ones.

As always, may we go in peace and gratitude, may we love and be loved fully and wonderfully in return, and may the Universe shower us with blessings.

Amen.

Our hymn for today, from the Broadway musical *Rent*, *Seasons of Love*. Let us sing.

What is your preferred love language? How might you use the information about Love Languages to improve an important relationship?

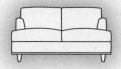

LOVE

Hello again, most brilliant and beloved Angels. Gather close as we figuratively join hands and join hearts to come together for a little while of quiet reflection.

With Valentine's Day close at hand, I come to you today to talk about love. Some of us may be anticipating sharing tokens of love and esteem, while others of us see the holiday looming on the horizon like a dark, glitter-covered Hallmark cloud. Not that I'm at all bitter.

The ancient Greeks, those smarties of yesteryear, thought of love as coming in many varieties. The first was eros, or sexual love. Their story goes that Cupid pierces us with his arrow, and we fall so madly in love, that the next thing you know, Troy falls because Paris had to have Helen. If anything captures our modern construct of romantic love, it is this. As wise person and ancient Greek poetess Sappho wrote . . .

Relaxing me from head to feet

Love masters me, the bitter sweet

O'er thy limbs breathing;

Yea, Eros now, the god born blind

Sweeps my soul like the mountain wind

Through the oaks seething.

I'll have what she's having indeed. Sometimes we get so focused on eros, or the lack thereof, that we lose sight of all the other yummy flavors. Like philia, the love we share with friends. It is said that William Penn named the city of brotherly love, Philadelphia, to commemorate his friendship treaty with the Lenape people. Rather than simply take the land through a charter from Charles II, he purchased the land directly from their chief. I'm not sure if it's true, but it would be lovely if it were.

Then there's agape, the unselfish and unconditional love we have for others. As wise person Rob Bell said, "Agape doesn't love someone because they're worthy. Agape makes them worthy by the strength and power of its love. Agape doesn't love somebody because they're beautiful. Agape loves in such a way that makes them beautiful." Have you heard of helper's high? Studies have shown that when we put agape into action, we can activate the same reward centers in our brains as drugs or food. That's what I call a win-win!

The Greeks called out three or four more kinds of love, but I'm going to end with the one that is often the most difficult for some of us—philautia, the love of one's self. As absolutely fabulous wise woman Lucille Ball said, "I have an everyday religion that works for me. Love yourself first, and everything else falls into line." It's not always easy, Dearest, I know. We've taken negative experiences and critical words too much to heart. But Steve Maraboli has some important advice: "Love yourself . . . enough to take the actions required for your happiness . . . enough to cut yourself loose from the drama-filled past . . . enough to set a high standard for relationships . . . enough to feed your mind and body in a healthy manner . . . enough to forgive yourself . . . enough to move on."

And so, dear Angels, I hope you will embrace all the kinds of love on Valentine's Day—especially loving yourself, flaws and all.

As always, may we go in peace and gratitude, may we know that we are loved and adored, and may the Universe shower us with blessings.

Amen.

Our hymn for today is *Love Make the World Go Round* by Lin-Manuel Miranda and Jennifer Lopez. Let us turn it up and shake a tail feather.

How do you feel about Valentine's Day? How can you show yourself a little love this week?

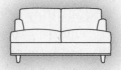

SAYING THE HARD THINGS

Hello again, most esteemed and enchanting Angels. Gather close as we figuratively join hands and join hearts to come together for a little while of some quiet reflection time.

I come to you today to talk about saying the hard things—specifically saying "I love you," "I'm sorry," or "I need help." A friend recently posted on social media asking which was the hardest one to say. So, I put it to you, Dearest, which one do you find to be the most difficult?

For some of us, saying I love you to another person literally strikes fear in our hearts. We may not have a lot of practice expressing our feelings. Maybe that wasn't something that was encouraged as we were growing up. Or the words remain frozen on our tongues because we fear the pain of rejection. Having had my heart broken to bits, I am all for proceeding with caution and self-preservation. To a point. But life is short, and I believe it is better to not leave these words unsaid, especially to family and friends. And none of this "me too," "thank you," or "ditto" nonsense. Because in the end, as wise person Barbara De Angelis said, "You never lose by loving. You always lose by holding back."

For others it is saying I'm sorry that gets stuck in our throats. Admitting that we caused damage and pain to another person is a difficult thing to come to terms with. It takes a great level of maturity to put yourself in that position of vulnerability and humility. Whisper it softly if you must but say the words. None of this "my bad," "sorry/ not sorry," or other non-apologies stuff. Sincerely express your remorse and offer to make amends by not repeating the past mistake. And for those on the receiving end, I'm a big fan of responding with something other than "it's okay." It's almost certainly not okay, but expressing acceptance helps us all heal. As wise person Donald L. Hicks said, "When you forgive, you free your soul. But when you say I'm sorry, you free two souls."

Lastly, we may have to work through a fear of asking for help. Full disclosure—this is the one I have to work on the most. Most of us like to think of ourselves as strong, competent, and independent. Maybe we're the ones who are used to helping others, so it feels uncomfortable to be on the other side. Then there's that fear of being in a vulnerable position again because your request may be rejected. But this is at the very heart of taking care of ourselves. I hate to break it to you—we're not superheroes. We are something infinitely more precious—fallible humans, with strengths and weaknesses. And we can remind ourselves of these wise words from Les Brown, "Ask for help. Not because you are weak. But because you want to remain strong."

If there is something today that you have left unsaid, I'm asking you to take a deep breath and a bold step today. Those hard words may be the key to make a change for the better.

As always, may we go in peace and gratitude, may we take the opportunity today to open our hearts and open our mouths to say what must be said, and may the Universe shower us with blessings.

Amen.

Today, we have double hymns! The first is *Words Don't Come Easy* as performed by Eleanor Kenny on YouTube, and *Help* by the Beatles. Let us sing.

> Which is the hardest for you to say? Is there one that needs to be said this week? If so, how will you do it?

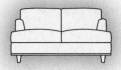

WONDERFUL YOU

Hello again, most amazing and attractive Angels. Gather close as we figuratively join hands and join hearts to come together for a little while of quiet reflection.

From time to time, I like to post little inspirational sayings on social media. And every time I do, folks say, in effect, that's a nice sentiment, but it's not about me. My heart breaks when I read those because, Dearest, it is indeed about all of us. All of our imperfections, zany quirks, and general weirdness makes us wonderfully human.

So why do we find it so hard to accept it when others pay us compliments or try to build us up? I had an aha moment reading an article by Zulie Rane. She said:

> It goes like this: you don't think much of yourself, for whatever reason. Maybe it's imposter syndrome, where you don't truly believe you belong. Maybe you've only been valued for one aspect for most of your life, like being smart, so it's impossible to see your worth in others, like being a good listener. Maybe you're continually comparing yourself to others and coming up short in your own estimation.
>
> Either way, you have low self-esteem. So, when someone compliments you, this jars with the truth

you hold about yourself. It's uncomfortable for your mind, because you're faced with two prospects: one, you're wrong about yourself, or two, they're lying. You can't simultaneously believe you suck and believe someone else when they say that you don't.

No one is born with low self-esteem. That comes from being bumped and bruised by our own poor thinking or the lies others told us. But that was the past. It's time now to let that garbage go. It's time to start caring for our emotional and physical health, to forgive where we can and ourselves most of all, and to remember that we are not our circumstances. Easier said than done, to be sure, but such important work.

Let's start with this advice from a wise anonymous person who said, "Insecurity knocks from time to time. Invite it in for a cup of coffee, talk with it, understand it. Then take that sugar spoon and poke it in the eye."

Next, let's practice something I had to learn myself—saying a simple "thank you" when someone pays you a compliment. No brushing it off. No discounting their words. So, I'm gonna throw some words on your amazing self. Ready?

- You are brave, strong, and smart. (Response: "Thank you.")

- You are a lovely person inside and out. (Response: "Thank you.")

- You are important, needed, and valued. (Response: "Thank you.")

Lather, rinse, repeat. Let it sink down into your spirit. Now you're ready for the advanced class—watch the video by Chris Hemsworth where he tells you how fabulous you are on a constant playback loop.

In the words of a wise anonymous person, "Everyone has inside them a piece of good news. The good news is you don't know how great you can be! How much you can love! What you can accomplish! And what your potential is." Believe it.

As always, may we go in peace and gratitude, may we recognize our worth, and may the Universe shower us with blessings.

Amen.

Our hymn for today is Alicia Keys's *Good Job* performed by the One Voice Children's Choir on YouTube. Let us sing.

How do you handle compliments? What, if anything, might you do to handle them in a new way this week?

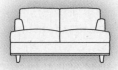

TIRED

Hello again, most radiant and ravishing Angels. Gather close as we figuratively join hands and join hearts to come together for a little while of quiet reflection.

I come to you today to talk about being tired. As an anonymous, wise, and witty person quipped, "I am not an early bird or a night owl. I am some form of permanently exhausted pigeon." And apparently, they're not the only ones. The average coffee drinker drinks 3.1 cups of coffee per day, and energy drink sales topped $3 billion in the US in 2018 alone. Sleep deficiency is rampant with 30–40 percent of adults getting less than the recommended hours required for rejuvenating our minds and bodies.

That is one side of the coin. The other is best summed up by wise person Mandeq Ahmed, who said, "There are two types of tired, I suppose. One is a dire need of sleep; the other is a dire need of peace." And sometimes both our bodies and spirits are weary.

We may all go through times in our lives when sleep is hard to come by—taking care of loved ones, trying to meet a deadline, or dealing with an emergency. But, Dearest, are you getting at least seven hours of sleep most nights? Sleeping less than that is associated with an increased risk of developing chronic conditions such as obesity, diabetes, high blood pressure, heart disease, stroke, and frequent mental distress, according to the CDC. In 2017 alone, 91,000 accidents were caused by drowsy driving.

As wise person Mesut Barazany said, "Your future depends on your dreams, so go to sleep." Turn off those blue-light devices, make your bedroom extra cozy, and develop a relaxing routine that lets your body know it's time for rest. If you're like me and your mind races like a rabid squirrel, put on a guided sleep meditation to help you relax. Maybe check in with a doctor if your sleeplessness is chronic.

For some folks, this will be the harder challenge— attaining the peace your spirit requires to feel rested. When we are soul weary, there's a good chance that we've let our boundaries slip. It's time to take a deep breath and say no. Say no to overscheduling your life. Say no to people guilting you into doing things. Say no to users and takers. You are nobody's doormat.

Perhaps we have let our worries get the best of us. As wise person Kahlil Gibran said, "Our anxiety does not come from thinking about the future, but from wanting to control it." This we know we cannot do.

Of course, just telling ourselves not to worry doesn't stop us from worrying. But we can put things in perspective, phone a friend, or throw some humor at it. In my family, we are all about keeping each other grounded. Dial the urgency up out of proportion, and you'll invariably hear, "Well, you did the first thing right. You hit the panic button." Insert eye roll here.

Carve out some time in your schedule, even if it's just 10 minutes, to blast some tunes and dance in the kitchen; snuggle with a pet or loved one; go for a walk and watch the sunset or stare at the stars; be as goofy and silly as you can. Touch base again with the things that make life worth living. This is the rest your soul needs, and it's important.

As always, may we go in peace and gratitude, may our minds and bodies feel rested and refreshed, and may the Universe shower us with blessings.

Amen.

Today's hymn is *Golden Slumbers* by the Beatles. Let us sing.

I f you are feeling physically tired, what is one thing you can do to get more sleep this week? If you are spiritually tired, what can you do to feel more refreshed?

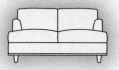

JOY

Hello again, most extraordinary and exquisite Angels. Gather close as we figuratively join hands and join hearts to come together for a little while of quiet reflection.

I come to you today to speak of joy—possibly the most powerful and lovely three-letter word there is. We may feel that joy is elusive, constantly scurrying just out of our reach. But in reality, and fair warning—this can be a tough one to accept—joy is a choice we make. As wise person Wes Stafford said, "Joy is a decision, a really brave one, about how you are going to respond to life."

Fortunately or unfortunately, the Universe will present many opportunities to practice this skill. Sometimes, it's life with a lower-case l. The car that won't start, the unexpected bill, the lost keys. Sometimes, it's the joy-sucking vampires in our lives. The unreasonable boss, the friend who says they hate drama but are actually a swirling vortex of chaos, the toxic family member. And sometimes, Dearest, it is life with a capital L. The loss, the negative diagnosis, a crushing expense.

How do we stop these things from stealing our joy? Well, as wise person Russell M. Nelson said, "The joy we feel has little to do with the circumstances of our lives and everything to do with our focus." And I really believe it is as simple and as frustratingly complicated as that.

For example, I've never been a morning person, but I had to get up by 5:30 A.M. every day for work. I hated it. But, in getting up that early, I got to see the silhouettes of the horses on the hills in the predawn light as I was driving to work, and that brought me joy.

When it comes to the people in our lives that suck the joy out of any room they are in, we have to make a conscious decision to set a boundary and be prepared to defend it. One of my favorite memes is the one with a guy holding out his hand saying, "Hey, train wreck. This isn't your station." I'm thinking it might be helpful to have a few T-shirts and a coffee mug with that imprinted on it.

Now we get to the hardest one—finding joy in our grief. I think it is critical to allow ourselves to experience the pain for a time without trying to pretend that all is well. But I think it is also important to try to find a tiny sliver of joy amid the ruins to prevent us from being crushed by the sadness. I heard a story about a woman who had just been diagnosed with cancer. She was, of course, devastated. That night, as she was getting into bed, her husband tenderly tucked her in, and she decided to focus on that moment of love and kindness instead.

And that, lovely Angels, brings me to the part where I commend us all to spread the joy around. We don't know the weight that others are carrying on their hearts. So, hold the door for someone, smile, do a favor, be free with your compliments. When they can't find their joy, you may be the one to hand them that precious gift. And who knows? Maybe in giving joy, a little may just bounce back on you.

As always, may we go in peace and gratitude, may we find and keep our joy come what may, and may the Universe shower us with blessings.

Amen.

Today's hymn is *Joy to the World* by Three Dog Night. Let us sing.

Who or what is stealing your joy? What is one positive thing you can do this week to be more joyful?

BOREDOM

Hello again, most splendid and spectacular Angels. Gather close as we once again figuratively join hands and join hearts to come together for a little while of quiet reflection.

I come to you today to talk about boredom. Like most teachers, one of the phrases that I have a low tolerance for is, "I'm bored." As wise one Viggo Mortensen once said, "There's no excuse to be bored. Sad, yes. Angry, yes. Depressed, yes. Crazy, yes. But there's no excuse for boredom, ever." In this day and age of the Internet, we have unlimited access to an infinite number of things to keep us entertained. Yet, in the immortal words of Bruce Springsteen, there are "fifty-seven channels and nothing on."

I believe, Dearest, that the root of the problem is a lack of desire to engage—we have a full menu in front of us, but nothing sounds good. Maybe we have a case of the blahs, feeling a little blue, or a lot depressed—we feel bored because we don't do anything new, and we don't do anything new because we feel bored. But there's a lot to be gained by moving forward. As wise person Oprah said, "Passion is energy. Feel the power that comes from focusing on what excites you."

The hardest part of overcoming that feeling of ennui is taking the first step. Use the buddy system if that step is too big on your own. Then pick a strategy to reset and repeat as often as necessary to jumpstart your joie de vivre.

- Water: drink it, bathe in it, swim in it, get near it. As wise science guy Wallace J. Nichols said, "Water . . . covers more than 70 percent of the Earth's surface, makes up nearly 70 percent of our bodies, and constitutes over 70 percent of our heart and brains. This deep biological connection has been shown to trigger an immediate response in our brains when we're near water. In fact, the mere sight and sound of water can induce a flood of neurochemicals that promote wellness, increase blood flow to the brain and heart, and induce relaxation."

- Go outside: feel the sun on your face, go for a walk, plant things in the dirt. Studies show that being outdoors, surrounded by nature and fresh air, increases energy by 90 percent. Professor Richard Ryan said, "Nature is fuel for the soul. Often when we feel depleted, we reach for a cup of coffee, but research suggests a better way to get energized is to connect with nature." It doesn't take much time—researchers found that being outdoors for just 20 minutes a day was enough to boost vitality levels.

- Mix it up: we sometimes get used to putting one foot in front of the other, caught up in our routines. Like a favorite song that's been overplayed, life can feel worn out and tired. As wise person Brian Stokes Mitchell said, "Variety is the key to not being bored." So, plan a surprise, try a new recipe, do a silly photo shoot. Give those creative muscles a much-needed workout.

As always, may we go in peace and gratitude, may we all feel a renewed zest for life, and may the Universe shower us with blessings.

Amen.

Today's hymn is *Fresh* by Kool and the Gang. Grab that sequined shirt from the back of the closet, get your groove on, and let us sing.

H ow do you deal with boredom? What new strategies might you try this week?

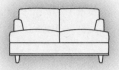

MIRACLES

Hello again, most wise and wonderful Angels. Gather close as we figuratively join hands and join hearts to come together for a little while of quiet reflection.

I come to you today to talk about a time when I was a little broken of spirit. For many years, I taught elementary school. One day, I had to file three child abuse reports on behalf of children who have only been on the planet for nine years. They told me of their suffering with hearts wide open in a roomful of other boys their age. Unfortunately, that wasn't the first time in 32 years that I had to file these reports, but it was the first time I had to do so many at once. Wrenching as it was, I also felt grateful to be in a position to help.

As I reflected on my experience and tried to make some sense of this world (and, full disclosure, contemplated dumping 50-gallon drums of whoop-ass on the ones who perpetrated this abuse), I managed to find some comfort in acknowledging that, while there seems to be no end to the cruelty that exists in this world, there is, too, an infinite number of everyday miracles that come into our lives.

I'm not talking about the life-altering breakthroughs or cures. Of course, those are awesome and inspire great rejoicing and gratitude. No, I'm talking about common, garden-variety miracles. As wise person Albert Einstein said, "There are only two ways to live your life. One is as though nothing is a miracle. The other is as though everything is a miracle."

But all too often, we get bogged down in our daily routines. Disappointments and losses can make us cynical and weary. What we need is an attitude adjustment, a refocus on the positive, a reframing of our outlook. As wise person Jon Bon Jovi said, "Miracles happen every day. Change your perception of what a miracle is, and you'll see them all around you."

Here's my list to get us started, Dearest. Feel free to add some of your own at the end.

- I'm alive and you're alive, and we're together in this place and time on this crazy, spinning, gorgeous Earth.

- The sun came up today, the moon will rise, and the stars will twinkle in the night sky.

- Babies smell divine, and their smiles and laughter are contagious.

- The sound of the waves crashing on the shore, the wind in your hair, and the sand between your toes can soothe your soul.

- Pets are the source of unconditional love and far better creatures than humans could ever hope to be.

- Family and friends who make us laugh and give us a shoulder to cry on.

- Music. From Alternative to Mariachi to Zydeco—all amazing and transformative.

- Every season has something breathtakingly beautiful about it.

- Random sneak attacks of kindness—given and received.

- But the greatest of these is love, in all its permutations, triumphs, and dogged persistence.

As always, may we go in peace and gratitude, may we find countless miracles along our paths, and may the Universe shower us with blessings.
Amen.

Today's hymn is *Ordinary Miracle* by Sarah McLachlan. Let us sing.

> What are the everyday miracles in your life that you are grateful for?

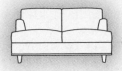

RAINBOWS

Good morning, most gracious and glorious Angels. Gather close as we figuratively join hands and join hearts to come together for a little while of quiet reflection.

Many years ago, I had the opportunity to go to Hawaii. What I knew about Hawaii then could have been best summed up as "corny honeymoon destination," but since my brother Matt was working there, I was game for a free place to crash on Oahu.

Those of you who have experienced the wonder first-hand truly understand how young and foolish I was back then, and those who haven't can still feel free to judge me. Once we left the hustle and bustle of Honolulu and arrived on the magical island of Kauai, I was in love. The beauty of the waterfalls, the lush greenery, the sound of the trade winds in the palm trees, and the crash of the waves on the beach. Sheer Heaven.

But there was something else that captivated me—the laid-back loveliness of the people. Everything was "no problem." When situations arose, they were handled, but there was no need to get your panties in a twist. What an amazing way to live. As wise person Paul Theroux said, "Hawaii is not a state of mind, but a state of grace."

I still have my favorite souvenir from that trip—a tie dyed T-shirt with the Hawaiian Rules printed on the back. For those of you not familiar with them, they are:

- Never judge a day by the weather.

- The best things in life aren't things.

- Tell the truth—there's less to remember.

- Speak softly and wear a loud shirt.

- Goals are deceptive—the unaimed arrow never misses.

- He who dies with the most toys still dies.

- Age is relative—when you're over the hill, you pick up speed.

- There are two ways to be rich—make more or desire less.

- Beauty is internal—looks mean nothing.

- No rain—no rainbows.

Each one of those babies is a sermon in itself, but I think they saved the best gem for last. So simple, yet so profound.

Now, I'm not 100 percent convinced that you have to know sadness to understand happiness or vice versa for that matter. And I think any one of us would gladly take a life filled only with joy if it were offered to us. But, as we know all too well, Dearest, no one is extending us that deal. For all the successes we have celebrated, we have despaired over our failures. For every new beginning, there was an ending. And perhaps the most difficult—grief is the price we pay for having had great love in our lives.

But how we deal with the rainy times will determine whether we get bitter or better. As wise person Adoniram Judson Gordon said, "Sorrow is only one of the lower notes in the oratorio of our blessedness." And with a name like Adoniram, you know you can take that to the bank. Knowing how easily things are lost or broken can help us be freer in expressing our gratitude. Those difficult times can also be a time of growth. As wise person Amy Poehler said, "Sometimes painful things can teach us things we didn't think we needed to know." So, if you're in a rainy season now, lean on the ones you love and be good to yourself. This, too, shall pass. You've survived 100 percent of your worst days so far. You've got this.

As always, may we go in peace and gratitude, may our rainbows outnumber the rain, and may the Universe shower us with blessings.

Amen.

Today's hymn is *Somewhere Over the Rainbow* performed by Israel "Iz" Kamakawiwo'ole. Let us sing.

Describe a time when you found a rainbow after the rain.

Part 2: Signs

YOU CAN ASK
THE UNIVERSE FOR
ALL THE SIGNS YOU
WANT, BUT ULTIMATELY
WE SEE WHAT WE WANT
TO SEE WHEN WE'RE
READY TO SEE IT.

— *How I Met Your Mother* (TV show)

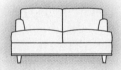

WAITING

Hello again, most sparkling and special Angels. Gather close as we figuratively join hands and join hearts to come together for a little while of quiet reflection.

I come to you today to talk about waiting. We spend much of our lives waiting. Sometimes we wish the time away—waiting to finish school, waiting for vacation, waiting to retire. Sometimes we wait in worry—for the test results, the verdict, the phone call. Sometimes we wait with hopeful expectation—for the birth of the baby, the sale to close, the plane to touch down.

These waiting times are never easy, but getting ourselves worked up about it sure is. We want so very badly to be in control of the situation or the outcome that we tie ourselves in knots. But, as wise person Dani Shapiro said . . .

> I don't know why this is, but I really believe that things don't happen when we're trying to will them into being. They don't happen when we're waiting for the phone to ring or the e-mail to pop up in our inbox. They don't happen when we're gripping too tightly. They happen—if they happen at all—when we've fully let go of the results. And, perhaps, when we're ready.

Then there are times when we wait to heal. Although it sounds like a load of crap when you're in the pit of despair, as a wise person once said, "Time heals all wounds." When we are grieving a loss, a heartbreak, a betrayal, the passage of time will eventually make the pain less sharp and the tears fewer. Many times, there is no getting over—just getting through.

So, my question to you, Dearest, is how will you spend the waiting times? There may be a season when you rail against the unfairness of the situation or shake your fists at how long it is taking. But we aren't meant to linger in that state. As wise one Joyce Meyer once said, "Patience is not an ability to wait, but the ability to keep a good attitude while waiting."

Easier said than done, to be sure. But there are some positive steps that you can take that may make this time productive. For your consideration . . .

- Attend to your health: drink water, get enough sleep, eat fresh foods, go for a walk, breathe

- Attend to your spirit: spend time in nature, explore various religions, keep a journal, see a therapist, do something you've never done before

- Attend to your intellect: learn something new by reading a book, taking a class, listening to a podcast

- Attend to the world outside yourself: give someone a ride, send a text, become an organ or blood donor, volunteer, send money

Full disclosure—writing these sermons has been a blessed way for me to spend my own waiting time. It's been a way for me to challenge myself, to connect with others, and to tap into my creative side.

As always, may we go in peace and gratitude, may we spend our waiting times in positive ways, and may the Universe shower us with blessings.

Amen.

Today's hymn is *The Waiting* performed by Eddie Vedder and Tom Petty and the Heartbreakers on YouTube. Let us sing.

Describe a waiting time in your life. What worked? What might you do differently next time?

MARIGOLDS

Hello again, most excellent and exceptional Angels. Gather close as we figuratively join hands and join hearts to come together for a little while of quiet reflection.

I come to you today to speak of plants—in particular marigolds and walnut trees. Although I retired from teaching, I still keep a lot of teacher-ish posts on my feed. While many of the stories still leave me with more classroom anxiety dreams than usual, one really resonated with me. Wise person Jennifer Gonzalez wrote an article in *Cult of Pedagogy* (yep, that's a thing) advising new teachers to seek out the "marigolds" and avoid the "walnut trees" at their school.

Why marigolds? Well, they are what expert gardeners call companion plants. These plants protect against pests and encourage growth, and marigolds are at the top of their game. In those places where we spend a significant amount of time, like home and work, it is important for us to find our nurturing companions. Those amazing folks are easy to spot. They are the ones who are free with their compliments; always have a tissue, band aid, or flask at the ready; and whose advice we seek out.

Once you have identified your marigolds, it's time for the next step. This is a hard one for independent folks—asking for support. Even the best of us need help from time to time. As wise person Barack Obama said, "To anyone out there who is hurting—it's not a sign of weakness to ask for help. It's a sign of strength." Start small if you must, but take that leap of faith. Marigolds are standing by, waiting for your call.

What if you've looked around only to find there's not a marigold in sight—just a bunch of weeds? Well then, Dearest, that is the Universe's way of letting you know that it is time for you to be the marigold. As wise person Robert Ingersoll said, "We rise by lifting others." So, hold the door, lend an ear, bake some cookies to share, or volunteer.

And to my most blessed marigolds out there, take some time for yourself. There's a fine line between being a helper and being a doormat. Set those boundaries, learn to say no, and put your oxygen mask on first.

But then, why walnut trees? While these trees provide excellent shade and tasty nuts, they contain a chemical called juglone. According to Purdue University, "Juglone has experimentally been shown to be a respiration inhibitor which deprives sensitive plants of needed energy for metabolic activity." So, plants growing in the vicinity will either be killed or will struggle to live. How's that for a scary-ass metaphor? Know someone who sucks the life out of a room? There's your walnut tree.

We can't always avoid the walnut trees, especially when they are in positions of authority. If this is the case, circle up your marigolds and find strength in numbers. If you can, run Forrest run. As wise person Kim McMillen said, "When I loved myself enough, I began leaving whatever wasn't healthy. This meant people, jobs, my own beliefs, and habits—anything that kept me small. My judgment called it disloyal. Now I see it as self-loving."

Here's the tough one—what if we're the walnut tree? Then Dearest, you must take the bravest step of all. Time for a deep breath. Examine your words and actions toward the ones nearest and dearest to you. Are they truly kind or just critical? Helpful or hurtful? Thoughtful or thoughtless? It's time to draw a line in the sand and say that this behavior ends today. It's time for your inner marigold to rise up and bloom.

Each one of us has the potential to either be a marigold or a walnut tree. The choice is ours every single day. Let us be intentional in our words and actions, erring always on the side of sweetness. As wise person Barbara De Angelis said, "Love and kindness are never wasted. They always make a difference. They bless the one who receives them and they bless you—the giver."

As always, may we go in peace and gratitude, may our paths be strewn with marigolds, and may the Universe shower us with blessings.

Amen.

Today's hymn is *I'll Be There for You* by the Rembrandts. Let us sing.

Who are the marigolds and walnut trees in your life?

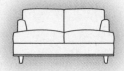

FEARLESS

Hello again, most marvelous and magnificent Angels. Gather close as we figuratively join hands and join hearts to come together for a little while of quiet reflection.

I come to you today to talk about fear and how it can hold us back from new and exciting experiences. How many times have we let fear keep us from stepping out or let it paralyze us into inaction? I know, Dearest, that very fear is protecting our tender hearts from being hurt again. But as wise person Marilyn Monroe said, "Just because you fall once doesn't mean you're gonna fail at everything."

We all have secret dreams, ones we keep safely tucked away and protected. But in locking those dreams away, not only do we miss the chance to live our lives fully, but we also deprive the world of our potential. As wise person Les Brown said,

> The graveyard is the richest place on earth, because it is here that you will find all the hopes and dreams that were never fulfilled, the books that were never written, the songs that were never sung, the inventions that were never shared, the cures that were never discovered, all because someone was too afraid to take that first step, keep with the problem, or determined to carry out their dream.

There are a few things we can do to make getting up on that high dive a bit easier. First, reframe your dream or goal into more than just an achievement—decide what you hope to learn from it. A concrete example might be interviewing for a new job. You may not get hired, but you might learn about other opportunities that the company has, how to sharpen your interview skills, or how to best promote yourself. At the risk of going all elementary school teacher on you, we teach the kids that FAIL = First Attempt in Learning. Cute, no?

Next, expect good things to happen, but don't pin all your hopes on the outcome. Thinking that we will die alone, surrounded by cats if the person we want to go out with rejects us, creates some pretty high stakes. If, instead, we go in with a positive attitude and decide to shrug it off if it doesn't go our way, then we can more easily bounce back and live to love another day.

Finally, remember your past successes—you have survived 100 percent of your worst days. It's not a whole lot of fun to deal with rejection and disappointment, but you're a badass, and you've made it this far. If it helps, blow the possible negative outcomes up to the point of being ridiculous and then decide how you would handle that situation. What if you decide to go to that open mic night and everyone points and laughs instead of cheering you on? Practice your snappiest comeback, complete with walking out of that dive in a huff. You are amazing—don't let anyone tell you otherwise.

If you knew you couldn't fail, what would you dare to do? As wise person W. Clement Stone said, "Thinking will not overcome fear, but action will." Take a brave step forward today—I'm rooting for you.

As always, may we go in peace and gratitude, may we make the leap, and may the Universe shower us with blessings.

Amen.

Today's hymn is *What If It All Goes Right?* by Melissa Lawson. Let us sing.

I f you knew you couldn't fail, what would you do? What could you do this week to move that dream forward?

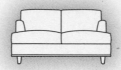

HEALING

Hello again, most lovely and luminous Angels. Gather close as we figuratively join hands and join hearts to come together for a little while of quiet reflection.

I come to you today to talk about healing, particularly healing from trauma. Many of us have been scarred from growing up in dysfunctional families, living in abusive relationships, or fighting to stay sane in crazy times. But I hope that going forward, we can start to heal for ourselves and for those around us. As a wise anonymous person said, "If you never heal from what hurt you, then you'll bleed on people who did not cut you."

I had read this powerful quote from wise person Catherine Woodiwiss a few months ago. Recently it came back to me, as beautiful words often do. She said . . .

Trauma permanently changes us. This is the big, scary truth about trauma: there is no such thing as "getting over it." The five stages of grief model marks universal stages in learning to accept loss, but the reality is, in fact, much bigger: a major life disruption leaves a new normal in its wake. There is no "back to the old me." You are different now—full stop. This is not a wholly negative thing. Healing from trauma can also mean finding new strength and joy. The goal of healing is not papering over changes in an effort to preserve or present things as normal. It is to acknowledge and wear your new life—warts, wisdom, and all—with courage.

Our mission, should we decide to accept it, is in becoming that new person, to become better not bitter. Sometimes we need more than just basic emotional first aid. Professionals may be needed to help us navigate. If that's the case, please don't wait to reach out.

There are a few things we can do on our own to help ease the pain, as suggested by Bay Area Mental Health, that I thought were particularly doable.

- Resources: identify resources within yourself or in your environment that make you feel safe, nurtured, and loved to help switch up your focus and rebuild your emotional foundation. Keep a funky right-brain journal to help you reflect and remember.

- Self-soothe: sometimes, we try to have others meet this need or go to bad places trying to help ourselves feel better. Instead, use your senses to find things that are beautiful to you—those are a potential source of soothing.

- Feel the feelings: scary, to be sure. As a wise person said, ignoring emotions is like banishing them to the basement, where they work out and get stronger and stronger until they erupt. Give yourself a limited amount of time to explore them—take baby steps.

- Express your feelings: when you name it and describe it, it loses some of its power.

- Integrate: put the parts together—resourcing, soothing, feeling, and expressing. You may alternate between different steps of the process many times as you work through whatever issues are holding you back.

Be patient. Healing rarely happens in a straight line. Give yourself plenty of credit and cut yourself plenty of slack. Remember that you are stronger than you know. And as a wise anonymous person said, "A scar simply means you were stronger than whatever tried to hurt you."

As always, go in peace and gratitude, may we get a little stronger with each day that passes, and may the Universe shower us with blessings.

Amen.

Today's hymn is *A Little Bit Stronger* by Sara Evans. Let us sing.

Where are you in the process of healing? What step forward feels doable this week?

DOUBTS

Hello again, most capable and charismatic Angels. Gather close as we figuratively join hands and join hearts to come together for a little while of quiet reflection.

I come to talk to you today about doubts—those niggling little thoughts that creep in and try their best to undermine us. As wise person and word wit William Shakespeare said, "Our doubts are traitors and make us lose the good we oft might win by fearing to attempt."

Sometimes, having a little doubt is a good thing. It can keep us from marrying the wrong person or getting caught up in a pyramid scheme. And, if we had 100 percent confidence in our talents and abilities, we would be prone to high-risk behaviors that could get us killed. Plus, that kind of thinking makes you the person no one wants to get stuck trying to make conversation with at a party. As wise person Oscar Wilde said, "Confidence is good, but overconfidence sinks the ship."

However, most of the time, doubt is what keeps us from taking the necessary bold steps forward to get what we want. Those annoying questions will pop into our minds—What if I make a fool of myself? What if I fail? What if I don't have the skills? What if I'm rejected? But, oh Dearest, what if you soar?

It's imperative, but certainly never easy, to drown out the internal and external critics. But wise person Chase Crawford offers this piece of advice: "Doubt your doubts before you doubt your beliefs." If you know in your heart of hearts that this is what you want, then you are going to have to reach deep inside for the courage to go forward. Lots of deep breaths. Do your prep work. Seek the advice and counsel of those who have gone before you. Round up a cheering section of your loved ones. And then tap into your inner trapeze artist—let go of the old and grab on to the new.

And if the worst happens and your effort is a total flop? Remind yourself that you've survived 100 percent of your worst days so far. Then, let these wise words from Winston Churchill inspire you to dust yourself off and snap that crown back into place: "Success is not final; failure is not fatal. It is the courage to continue that counts."

As always, may we go in peace and gratitude, may we remember how brave we truly are, and may the Universe shower us with blessings.

Amen.

Today's hymn is *I'm a Believer* performed by the Monkees. Grab your bell bottoms and your tambourine and let us sing.

Describe a time when you overcame your doubts. What lesson(s) did you learn from this experience?

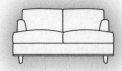

POTENTIAL

Hello again, most divine and delightful Angels. Gather close as we figuratively join hands and join hearts to come together for a little while of quiet reflection.

I come to you today to talk about potential—that powerful word that's all about the future and what it could hold in store for each and every one of us. Because, Dearest, I believe you have an assignment here, a destiny if you will, that only you can fulfill.

For many of us, it is a challenge just to put one foot in front of the other each day—to go to work, pay the bills, take care of loved ones. Our daily responsibilities can weigh heavily on our shoulders. We become weary, and our days become routinized. (By the way, if you haven't seen the Disney short "Inner Workings," I highly recommend it. It's the perfect illustration of my point with a feel-good ending.)

So, how do we break free and tap into our higher purpose? First, you have to carve out some time for yourself. I know I get preachy on self-care, but it really is the first step of any journey. When you get quiet, mull things over. Your heart has a wisdom all its own. You may have known all along what you were meant to do. I knew since I was in second grade that I wanted to be a teacher. Or you may stumble upon it one day like I did in writing these sermons. But there's no time like the present to find out. As wise person Eric Thomas said, "You cannot afford to live in potential for the rest of your life. At some point, you have to unleash the potential and make your move."

So, write things down—some ideas, dreams, and goals. No matter how unrealistic they may seem. In fact, sometimes, the most improbable ones are the best. If you could achieve it now, it wouldn't be potential. As wise person C. S. Lewis said, "You are never too old to set a new goal or to dream a new dream."

Next, think of one or two baby steps forward that you could take. You may need to learn more things or practice what you've been doing on a more regular, intentional schedule. Write that down too. Better yet—put it on your calendar for this week.

Then, find a mentor or a group who can offer advice and guidance. If you are the smartest person in your group, your group is too small. The Internet awaits—look for a page that can help. Ladies interested in running for office should check out Emily's List. Want to write? Go to Camp NaNoWriMo and check out their online writers' camp. Interested in starting your own business? Visit the federal Small Business Administration website.

Lastly, don't give up. We all have times when it's two steps forward and one step back. Maybe we even have people in our lives who've told us we can't. As wise person Rumi said, "You were born with potential. You were born with goodness and trust. You were born with ideals and dreams. You were born with greatness. You were born with wings. You are not meant for crawling, so don't. You have wings. Learn to use them and fly."

As always, may we go in peace and gratitude, may our wildest dreams come true, and may the Universe shower us with blessings.

Amen.

Today's hymn is *I Can Do Hard Things* by Jennifer Nettles. Let us express some gratitude for all the strong women in our lives and let us sing.

H ow would you describe your potential? How might you release more of your potential this week?

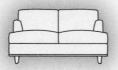

GARBAGE TRUCKS

Hello again, most savvy and scintillating Angels. Gather close as we figuratively join hands and join hearts to come together for a little while of quiet reflection.

I come to you today to share a story I heard. One day, wise person David J. Pollay was in a taxi on his way to the airport when suddenly a car whipped in and cut them off. The quick-thinking driver slammed on his brakes and narrowly avoided an accident. And did the driver at fault wave apologetically and thank the Universe that no one was hurt? Why, no, friends! Being the giant douche catamaran that he was, he started yelling at the taxi driver.

And did the taxi driver give a one-fingered salute and yell back? No, friends. Being a much better person than I am, he smiled and waved at the other driver. Astonished, Pollay asked why he was so positive. The most wise driver said, "Many people are like garbage trucks. They run around full of garbage, full of frustration, full of anger, and full of disappointment. As their garbage piles up, they need a place to dump it, and sometimes they'll dump it on you. Never take it personally. Just smile, wave, wish them well, and move on with the routine life."

So, Angels, I believe there are some important take-aways here. First, we may be surrounded by garbage trucks—strangers, co-workers, and sadly, family and friends. With strangers, let us strive to be like the taxi driver. It's not always easy to ignore bad behavior, but as a wise anonymous person said, "The less you respond to negative people, the more positive your life will become." Do it for your own peace if nothing else.

But what if it's those in our inner circle? Are they just having a bad day and need a little slack? We all have those days when we hope for understanding and comfort. On the other hand, and more importantly, is it a pattern of behavior? If that is the case, it's time to take a long, hard look at how they are treating you. As wise person Tony Gaskins said, "You teach people how to treat you by what you allow, what you stop, and what you reinforce." You are the Universe's most wondrous creation, not a garbage dump.

And now, Dearest, it is time to take an honest look at ourselves. Are we handling our frustrations, anger, and disappointments by spewing garbage on everyone in our path? If that has been the case, we need to draw a line in the sand and start making amends today. As wise person Yehuda Berg said, "Hurt people hurt people. That's how pain patterns get passed on, generation after generation. Break the chain today." It may take some time to change—old habits die hard, and you can't earn back trust overnight. But it is oh so worth it.

As wise ones Marc and Angel Chernoff remind us, "Those times when you don't feel like being positive are the times when choosing to be positive makes the biggest difference."

As always, may we go in peace and gratitude, may our paths be clear of garbage trucks, and may the Universe shower us with blessings.

Amen.

Today's hymn is *Humble and Kind* by Tim McGraw. Let us sing.

Who are the garbage trucks in your life? How will you deal with them in a more positive way this week?

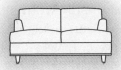

TAKE COURAGE

Hello again, most intuitive and irresistible Angels. Gather close as we figuratively join hands and join hearts to come together for a little while of quiet reflection.

I come to you today to talk about discouragement— that beat-down feeling we all experience when nothing seems to be going our way. That no matter how hard we look, our spark of hope seems nowhere to be found. However, in the wise words of Court Young, "Being discouraged is natural, but giving up is not an option."

So how to hokey pokey and turn ourselves around? Some of us are lucky to have cheerleaders in our lives who are always good for a pep talk. Those folks are a blessing. But sometimes it's up to us to remind ourselves that we have survived 100 percent of our worst days and that nevertheless, we will persist. A wise anonymous source says, "Let discouragement harden your determination, never your heart."

Many times, discouragement comes from a misalignment of our expectations with reality. We want our timelines for success to be shorter than they usually are. We want to lose 10 pounds in a week, instantly meet our soul mate, pay off our debts in a minute. Most of the time, life doesn't work that way. But the funny thing is that once you are over the hump of achieving your goal, the time you spent getting there doesn't usually feel that long. And the effort usually feels totally worth it. So, tell yourself the stories of all the times you made it and remind yourself what it took to get there. If you don't have stories, make some up that help you gain perspective. I'll never know.

Self-care is an important and universal step in the right direction. No one can tackle the world on low blood sugar and sleep deprivation. So, hydrate, eat fresh foods, go for a walk, and get some solid rest. Distance yourself from toxic people whenever possible. Set some personal boundaries to carve out some space for yourself. Put your oxygen mask on first.

Another step that helps us get on the right track in a variety of situations is doing for others. Can you be that cheerleader for someone else? Can you be a mentor and share those mad skills you've mastered? Is there a cause in a different direction that can help you to stop dwelling on your disappointments? As wise person Oprah said, "To move forward, you have to give back."

I found these wise words from Paul A. Adefarasin deeply comforting . . .

Somewhere in the inner recesses of every heart, hidden beneath layers of pain and discouragement, rejection and abuse, destiny calls. It is a call from your future, the call from eternity. It beckons you to a destiny that will not die. There are some who will live and die in the deserts of life, never quite reaching the point of their destiny. There are yet others who, with relentless determination, will press beyond their limitations as they reach for the prize of their promise.

If you feel a stirring in your spirit when you read that, that's the flicker that can turn into a flame. As eminently wise person William Shakespeare said, "Screw your courage to the sticking-place, and we'll not fail."

As always, may we go in peace and gratitude, may we reach for the prize of our promise, and may the Universe shower us with blessings.

Amen.

Our hymn for today is *High Hopes* by Panic at the Disco. Let us sing.

W hat is one goal you are proud to have achieved? How did you achieve it?

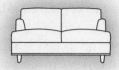

CROSSROADS

Hello again, most talented and terrific Angels. Gather close as we figuratively join hands and join hearts to come together for a little while of quiet reflection.

I come to you today to tell you a story I heard about famed architect Frank Lloyd Wright. It seems, as a boy, he was walking across a snow-covered field with his uncle. As nine-year-old boys are wont to do, he meandered here and there, looking at things that caught his interest while his uncle, apparently a buttoned-up sort of fellow, made a beeline for the far side of the field. When they met back up, the uncle took the opportunity to impart his wisdom to the boy. "Notice how your tracks wander aimlessly from the fence to the cattle to the woods and back again," his uncle said. "And see how my tracks aim directly to my goal. There is an important lesson in that."

When he grew up, Wright liked to tell how this experience had greatly contributed to his philosophy in life. "I determined right then," he'd say with a twinkle in his eye, "not to miss most things in life, as my uncle had."

Some of us are like the uncle—we find efficiency and task completion to be very satisfying and rewarding. All the items checked off a to-do list is a little slice of Heaven. A place for everything and everything in its place is part of our enduring motto. Nothing wrong with that. As wise person Dr. T. P. Chia said, "To be successful is to be goal-oriented, diligent, determined, persistent, and persevering."

Some of us are like the boy—we take joy in the journey, not the destination. Leaving the map behind and exploring the backroads while losing all track of time is fulfilling. Those wise words of J. R. R. Tolkien are tattooed on our spirit: "Not all those who wander are lost." Nothing wrong with that either. To paraphrase wise person Anatole France, "Wandering re-establishes the original harmony which once existed between us and the universe."

As with all things in life, it's about the balance. If we enjoy having a roof over our heads and food on the table, we have to take care of our responsibilities like showing up for work and paying our bills on time. Most folks don't dream of taking in a freeloader who needs to ground themselves by traipsing through the forest barefoot by day and nuding it up to take moon baths by night.

On the other hand, not many people want to be in the company of people who can't ever deviate from a schedule, slip coasters under every drink, and overthink the pros and cons of every item on a menu. As an anonymous wise person said, "Some days you eat salads and go to the gym. Some days you eat cupcakes and refuse to put on pants. It's called balance."

So, Dearest, take a walk on the wild side and go someplace near or far that you've never been. Order something you've never tried before at that new place in town. Go dancing in the middle of the week. Or go shopping with a list and stick to it. Buy tickets for an event that's months away. Catch up on all those appointments you've been procrastinating over for months. Be true to who you are, but see what's on the other side of the fence.

As always, may we go in peace and gratitude, may we strike the perfect balance this week, and may the Universe shower us with blessings.

Amen.

Today's hymn is *Crossroads* by Tracy Chapman.
Let us sing.

Are you more like the boy or more like the uncle? What can you do this week to try out a different approach?

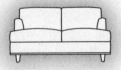

PERMISSION

Hello again, most real and resourceful Angels. Gather close as we figuratively join hands and join hearts to come together for a little while of quiet reflection.

I come to you today to talk about giving yourself permission. When we were young, we probably had to ask for permission to do just about anything—have a friend over, borrow the car, stay out late. In adulthood, acting on our autonomy to give ourselves permission becomes a challenge. We have to figure out when we are free to act on our own and when we have to have the approval of an authority figure—all without an instruction manual.

As a young adult, I think I often worried that I would "get in trouble" if I took a bold step outside the lines. During that time, I think one of the best pieces of advice I ever received is, "It's easier to ask forgiveness than permission." It is one to apply with caution, but it has helped me take brave steps forward when I knew in my heart that it was right to go ahead, and I could deal with the consequences after the fact. As wise person Richelle E. Goodrich said, "What do you mean I have to wait for someone's approval? I'm someone. I approve. So, I give myself permission to move forward with my full support!"

Now, Dearest, if this is out of your comfort zone, my advice would be to start small. Give yourself permission for some self-care, like having a lazy day and staying in your pajamas. Feel that niggling sensation of guilt? That's just years of nonsensical cultural programming trying to have its way. In a loud, clear voice tell it, "Not today, Satan!", shake it off, and let the binge watching, binge reading, and binge napping begin.

For those intermediate swimmers, it's time to paddle out to the deeper end of the pool and start giving yourself permission to take a bold step of faith into something new. Or to not be perfect at everything every time. Or to have a good, long cry.

And for those ready for the advanced class, ready to jump off the high dive? What about giving yourself permission to ask for what you want in a relationship? Or to ask for help? Or to release the past and start over? Or to forgive yourself for the times you really screwed up?

I'm not saying it's easy. In fact, in some cases, it may be the hardest thing you've ever done. But I do think it's worth it. As wise person Valerie Tarico said, "It's difficult to describe the peace that comes with giving yourself permission to know what you know. To have hard, complicated realities staring at you and be able to raise your head and look back at them with a steady gaze, scared maybe, grieved perhaps, but straight on and unwavering."

Let us march into the coming week with these words of advice from a wise anonymous person who said, "Give yourself permission to live a big life. Step into who you are meant to be. Stop playing small. You're created for greater things."

As always, may we go in peace and gratitude, may we trust ourselves enough to grant ourselves permission in things great and small, and may the Universe shower us with blessings.

Amen.

Today's hymn is *My Prerogative* performed by Parlor Social on YouTube. Let us swing it and sway it and let us sing.

What will you give yourself permission to do this week? How does that feel?

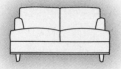

TRUST

Hello again, most loved and lovable Angels. Gather close as we figuratively join hands and join hearts to come together for a little while of quiet reflection.

I come to you today to talk about pistanthrophobia. What the what, you say? Pistanthrophobia is the fear of trusting others based on past experiences. If you've spent any time here on planet Earth, you probably have at least a touch of it. And while a healthy dose of skepticism can keep us from physical and emotional harm, too much can keep us stunted and alone.

Now, Dearest, I know that this world can be an unpredictable dumpster fire, filled with rogues and scoundrels waiting to take advantage of a kind and gentle heart. After repeated exposure to these villains, our world view becomes clouded until we feel like we must be on constant high alert. But as an anonymous wise person said, "How do you know who to trust when human hearts are never readable? You must understand that trust is not a function of full knowledge but a readiness to take risks."

So, it starts with us. It starts with trusting ourselves, to have confidence that even if our trust is betrayed, we have the strength and the courage to survive it. After all, if you're reading this, you have survived 100 percent of your worst days so far. Forgive yourself for trusting the wrong people—that is a reflection on their poor choices, not on you. What happened in the past does not have to determine your future.

If we are to be able to trust ourselves, we must take a long, hard look in the mirror to see if we are, in fact, trustworthy people. Do we honor our commitments? Do we respect confidences? Are we honest? Can we be counted on to come through for our family and friends when they need us? If the sincere answer to any of these questions is no, I say this with love—it's time to do better.

Then, start listening to your intuition—that still, small voice inside your heart and head that is meant to protect and guide you. Too often, we ignore the warning signs that are trying to keep us safe. As wise person Dr. Benjamin Spock (No, not the guy from *Star Trek*. The famed pediatrician.) said, "Trust yourself. You know more than you think you do." If something doesn't feel quite right, it probably isn't.

Once we have our own house in order, we can begin the brave journey of learning to trust others. In order to do that, we have to give them ample time to show us who they are. The problem is, we get swept up in our emotions and often rush the process. Then at some point, we will just have to take the leap. Although he's not my favorite author, Ernest Hemmingway wisely said, "The best way to find out if you can trust somebody is to trust them." Start with small things that have low risk—ask for little favors or some advice. Be sure you are loving and trusting the actual person, not just the person they have the potential to be.

Dear Angels, I hope I never give the impression that I have things all figured out, 'cuz I have my own faults and foibles like everybody else. For example, I'm used to being a very independent person, and I have a hard time asking for help. (My brothers just collectively cracked up because I frequently call on them when it's time to move.) I realize this is a trust issue for me—I'm afraid that someone will say no, and I don't like feeling vulnerable and rejected. With my brothers, it's easier. We've known each other for always and I trust them, not only with my life, but also not to break too much of my crap.

Look around you—who can you count on to have your back? If you can't find anyone, then the Universe is telling you to start with yourself and slowly build your circle. As wise person Sushant Kaushik said, "Trust is not easy, but living without trust is even harder."

As always, may we go in peace and gratitude, may we trust and be trusted in return, and may the Universe shower us with blessings.

Amen.

Today's hymn is *Count on Me* performed by Whitney Houston and CeCe Winans. Let us sing.

What are your thoughts about trusting yourself and/or others? Are there any positive changes you are considering for the week ahead?

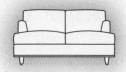

KARMA

Hello again, most sweet and strong Angels. Gather close as we figuratively join hands and join hearts to come together for a little while of quiet reflection.

I come to you today to talk about karma. Now, I'm no expert, but I've learned a few things. Here in the West, we often talk about karma as some sort of divine retribution, but it's more complex than that. (Imagine— oversimplifying a complex concept in order to create a joke or hilarious meme!) In many Eastern philosophies, there is no cosmic judge that rewards "good" or punishes "bad" behavior, so there really isn't such a thing as good or bad karma.

The root of the word *karma* comes from the Sanskrit word kri: क्र. It means "to do" or "to act." Wise person Buddha described karma as "this arises, that becomes." While there is a relationship between cause and effect, it's more of a circular construct than a law.

Now that we've cleared that up, and I've had an opportunity to flex my elementary teacher muscles, it's time to share the cool part of what I stumbled upon—12 tenets of karma. Some folks refer to them as laws, but really, they're more like lessons.

1. The Great Law: Whatever we put into the Universe will come back to us.

2. The Law of Creation: Life does not happen by itself—we have to make it happen.

3. The Law of Humility: We must accept something before we can change it.

4. The Law of Growth: By changing ourselves, we change our lives.

5. The Law of Responsibility: We are responsible for what happens in our lives.

6. The Law of Connection: The past, the present, and the future are all connected.

7. The Law of Focus: We cannot think of two different things at the same time.

8. The Law of Giving and Hospitality: Our behavior should match our thoughts and actions.

9. The Law of Here and Now: We cannot be present if we are looking backward.

10. The Law of Change: History repeats itself until we learn from it and change our path.

11. The Law of Patience and Reward: The most valuable rewards require persistence.

12. The Law of Significance and Inspiration: Rewards are a result of the effort and energy we put into them.

Like the Hawaiian Rules I shared before, each one of these gems could be a sermon on its own. Each one of you reading this will take away something different and beautifully personal. For me, it's the theme of time—how the past, present, and future are all connected to each other and to us. I'm also particular to the first one. As wise person Peyton Conway March said, "There is a wonderful mythical law of nature that the three things we crave most in life—happiness, freedom, and peace of mind—are always attained by giving them to someone else."

I think, Dearest, this is why we are here—life presents us with lessons that we get to practice over and over until we learn them; we need to make amends when we cause hurt, and we are to put as much good into the world as we possibly can in the short time we're given.

As always, may we go in peace and gratitude, may we pass our lessons easily the first time, and may the Universe shower us with blessings.

Amen.

Today's hymn (because I just couldn't resist) is *Karma Chameleon* by Culture Club. Grab your eyeliner and let us sing.

Which of these laws resonates most with you? Why?

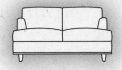

ANCHORS

Hello again, most charming and cherished Angels. Gather close as again we figuratively join hands and join hearts to come together for a little while of quiet reflection.

From time to time, when the world gets crazy, we can all experience feeling disoriented. So many times, I have felt tossed about like a tiny ship in a big storm. It got me to thinking about ways to steady myself and hold fast to reality amid the madness. So, in keeping with this nautical metaphor, I come to you today to talk about anchors—those lovely old symbols that represent stability, strength, and support.

As wise person Clare Milliken explained, "An anchor is something that grounds you in yourself—your mind and your body. An anchor is something you can hold on to when you feel overwhelmed. An anchor is something that makes you feel calmer, more at ease, and more sure of yourself. Anchors can take many forms, and what works at one time may not work in another instance."

From the beginning, people have held on to amulets, talismans, and lucky charms of all kinds to give them a sense of security and confidence. Ancient Egyptians had their ankhs, and Christians, Muslims, and Jews have their hamsas. Even modern folk have a penchant for them. Vida Blue, a famous pitcher with the Oakland As in the '70s and '80s had a favorite cap. He wore it until it was so shabby that league officials threatened to suspend him if he didn't remove it. Madonna once said, "Britney Spears became my talisman. I became obsessed with wearing Britney T-shirts. I felt it would bring me luck. And it did."

Anchors can be visual, auditory, or physical. Anything that evokes a sense of calm will do. Some folks already carry a little token around with them, but if you need some suggestions, consider these:

- Visual: a picture of a loved one or a special place, ticket stub, book of matches, receipts
- Auditory: a favorite song, nature sounds, a voice message
- Physical: jewelry, stones, shells, coins, blankets, clothing, coffee mugs

Routines and special family events can serve as anchors as well. Taco Tuesdays, movie, game, or date nights, Sunday brunch—all can give us something positive to look forward to and count on even when life gets crazy. As wise person Ray Boltz said, "The anchor holds in spite of the storm."

So, Dearest, when the road gets rocky, let us see if touching base with a beloved special something can't help us feel a little more sure of ourselves, take us back to a happy remembered time, and ground us until we can get our bearings again.

As always, may we go in peace and gratitude, may we hold on for another day, and may the Universe shower us with blessings.

Amen.

Today's hymn is *Hold On* performed by Sweet Suspense on YouTube. Let their joy be contagious and let us sing.

What types of anchors do you have in your life? Which anchors might you add?

Part 3: Wonders

WONDER
IS THE BEGINNING
OF WISDOM.

— Socrates

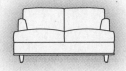

CHANGE

Hello again, most adored and adorable Angels. Gather close as we figuratively join hands and join hearts to come together for a little while of quiet reflection.

I come to you today to talk about change. Does that word spark excitement and the possibility of new adventures? Or trepidation about the future and a feeling of solid ground shifting beneath your feet? I have to admit that I'm more likely to feel fearful when facing change. But as wise person Benjamin Disraeli said, "Change is inevitable. Change is constant." Other wise people might respond, "Thanks for nothing, Ben."

There seem to be a few flavors of change. First are the changes we choose—changes that may take some adjusting to, but nevertheless, can be counted on to bring us new experiences, positive growth, and bright beginnings. Earning that promotion, getting married, having a baby, traveling somewhere we've never been. Of course, we're excited, but we can also feel stressed or even experience dread. Having your feelings mixed up can be discombobulating as all get-out.

A few years ago, I moved into a new place. It was more spacious and modern, and the landlord was waaaay cooler. When my friends helped me move in, they sang the theme song from The Jeffersons, *Movin' On Up* (Google it, kids). I should have been ecstatic, but I was oddly depressed. Then I realized—I was grieving my old place. The old gas stove like my grandparents had, the shorter commute, the memories I had made there. While I didn't necessarily want to go back, I missed it. It took me months to get over the funk. And even now, there are times when I fondly think back to living there.

Then there are the changes that knock us to our knees—whether we see them coming or they hit us out of the blue. Like when the rug gets pulled out from under us when we lose a loved one, go through a breakup, or receive a negative diagnosis. After teaching for 15 years, I had the opportunity to work at the district level, coordinating programs and supporting teachers. I wrote grants that brought in over $1 million and built new community relationships. My refusal to comply with what I felt was an unethical practice was the beginning of the end of that position, and I was sent back to the classroom. Most days, when I was laughing with my students or when they ran up to give me a hug, that upset felt miles away. But every once in a while, I feel that pang of unfairness all over again.

So, if you're anything like me and feel that good and bad changes can both well and truly suck—then what is to be done? As I was writing this sermon, a wise person (who upon further research was apparently not Buddha) laid a heavy truth right upside my head by saying, "Change is never painful. Only resistance to change is painful." So clearly, there is an element of attitude adjustment and working toward acceptance. Also, whenever I have the chance, I'm going to advocate for self-care, so eat right, stay hydrated, get enough sleep, seek help, and find positive outlets for your feelings. And, above all else, be gentle and loving with yourself as you go through the process.

And, Dearest, if you are in an unhealthy or abusive situation, I know that change can seem almost impossible. But, as wise person Bryant McGill said, "Escaping a toxic relationship can feel like breaking a piece of your heart off; like a wolf chews off his leg to escape a steel trap. Leaving is never easy, but sometimes it's necessary to save yourself and others from dying inside." Please don't wait to make the change.

As always, may we go in peace and gratitude, may change be a positive force in our lives, and may the Universe shower us with blessings.

Amen.

Today's hymn is *I Wanna Go Back* by Eddie Money. Let us sing.

How do you feel about change? What strategies work best for you when dealing with these times of flux?

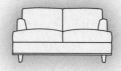

GRACE

Hello again, most grand and generous Angels. Gather close as we figuratively join hands and join hearts to come together for a little while of quiet reflection.

I come to you to talk about grace—such a lovely, nuanced word. As this sermon was percolating in my brain, I was focused on one meaning, but ever so many more have bubbled up to the surface.

The first meaning that came to mind was that grace is freely given, unmerited love. Now, Dearest, I want to assure you first and foremost that you are always deserving of deep and abiding love because sometimes we forget. We feel as though we're just too flawed, too damaged. Grace is when we know that we are cherished in spite of, or maybe even because of, our human propensity to fall short of perfection. Know that even when you may not receive grace from the people around you, the Universe is surrounding you with unconditional love.

We can also have the power of being on the giving side of grace every time we embrace another when they sincerely and without malice stumble on their journey. As wise person Heather K. O'Hara said, "Do everything with gentleness, with kindness, with reverence. That is how grace moves. That is how love dances."

Grace can also be an expression of thanks offered up before a meal. We appreciate all the love and work that went into getting our food from its source to our table and the fact that we have enough when others don't. Grace and gratitude go hand in hand, whether we are in the light times or in the dark times. As wise person Oprah said, "When you meet obstacles with gratitude, your perception starts to shift, resistance loses its power, and grace finds a home within you."

Sometimes we think of grace in terms of being unflappable—of having grace under fire. Those times when we dig way down and find that well of strength that resides within each of us, hold our head up high, and assert, "Not today, Satan!" with a snap and a hair flip. You may be a little rusty, but trust me—you have it in you. As wise person Ann Voskamp reminds us, "Grace is the weapon that disarms the dark."

Finally, we come to grace as a description of carrying oneself with confidence and poise. I'm here to tell you, Angels, that while I have some good qualities, being genteel and graceful ain't any of them. I can trip over my own two feet and will spit out my beverage if you make me laugh hard enough. But rather than fret about my lack of Audrey Hepburn-like carriage, I will take comfort in these wise words from Dana Dalgetty, who said, "Kindness is grace and grace is elegance." We may not have the moves like Jagger, but we can all be kind.

In difficult times, I think we can all use a little more grace in our lives, no matter what form it takes—a warm embrace, a moment of thanksgiving, a surge of courage when we need it most, or being able to stride through a restaurant without leaving spilled drinks and broken glass in our wakes. I'll leave you with the words of wise woman

Anne Lamott: "I do not at all understand the mystery of grace—only that it meets us where we are but does not leave us where it found us."

As always, may we go in peace and gratitude, may grace find us at every turn, and may the Universe shower us with blessings and humor.

Amen.

Today's hymn is *Hallelujah* performed by Pentatonix. As all the good feels wash over us, let us sing.

What comes to mind when you hear the word *grace*?

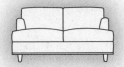

WORRY

Hello again, most blessed and breathtaking Angels. Gather close as we figuratively join hands and join hearts to come together for a little while of quiet reflection.

I come to you today to talk about worry—those times when anxiety gets the best of us, and our minds go to the bad place. Often thoughts will come to us about things that may befall us or our loved ones. Things that shake our foundation of security to the core. We allow our minds to run through a million scenarios about every possible, and even a few impossible, things that could happen.

In life, so many of the things that we worry about never actually happen. How many of us can reflect back on times we worried about not getting into school, a bad job review, or a negative diagnosis that never came to pass? All that wasted time and energy. As wise person Robert Downey Jr. said, "Worrying is like praying for something that you don't want to happen."

My experience has been that it's never the things that we worry about that knock us to our knees. Although I'm not a Monty Python fan, I have always found, "No one ever expects the Spanish Inquisition" to be both morbidly funny and oddly comforting. The unexpected death, the person who leaves without warning, the disaster that strikes out of the blue—we didn't even think to worry about those situations, and yet here they are.

And then there are those times in life when exactly what we worried about did come to be. But, in those moments, after all the dread, you may find that you, in fact, do have the strength to face the worst. You are mightier than you know, Dearest. You have survived 100 percent of your very worst days. And, as a darling creation of the Universe, you have all the love and support you need, supplied in abundance. Know deep in your spirit, that no matter how hard it may be, you will overcome whatever you need to.

And for those Zen masters out there, I offer this challenge—turn your worry into wonder. Instead of worrying about the interview, wonder about how much money they'll offer you to work there. Instead of worrying about past mistakes, wonder how bright your future will be. How much less anxiety and stress could we have if we could reframe our worry?

None of this is easy. If only a gentle scolding to stop worrying would do the trick! But it helps, I think, to put it in perspective. Perhaps the best wisdom I found came from Corrie ten Boom, the brave woman who, along with her family, helped hide Jews from the Nazis in their home. She said, "Worrying is carrying tomorrow's load with today's strength—carrying two days at once. It is moving into tomorrow ahead of time. Worrying doesn't empty tomorrow of its sorrow; it empties today of its strength."

As always, may we go in peace and gratitude, may we find our place of calm in the storm, and may the Universe shower us with blessings.

Amen.

Today's hymn is *Don't Worry, Be Happy* by Bobby McFerrin. Let us smile as we sing.

What are you worrying about today? What are some positive ways you can deal with it this week?

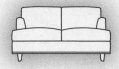

WORTHY

Hello again, most caring and clever Angels. Gather close as we figuratively join hands and join hearts to come together for a little while of quiet reflection.

I come to you today to talk about worthiness. Not long ago, I reposted a cartoon on social media in which a person asks a genie for a wish—to be worthy of love. The genie, with a flourish, announces, "It is done." The person argues that nothing has changed, to which the genie replies, "That is correct." It's one of my favorites—four simple panels that remind us of a profound truth. Like the tin man with his heart, the scarecrow with his brain, and the lion with his courage, we've had it all along.

And while some people respond positively, every time I post the cartoon, I get a couple of different responses that break my heart. The first are the ones that attempt to make a joke. Now, I love nothing more than to have a good laugh, but Dearest, in this case, that is a defense mechanism to mask the pain. The second is that while they wish they could believe it, it could not possibly be true for them.

I'm not vain or naive enough to think that a few words from me could possibly take away all the hurt and convince someone to acknowledge their inherent worthiness, as much as I might want to. That has to come from within, often with the help of a trusted mental health guide. But my hope is that I might offer up some thoughts for consideration.

The first is that we came into this world worthy. As Lady Gaga would say, we were born this way. Dignity, respect, and love were part of our birthright simply because we had a heartbeat and drew breath—it was never something we had to earn. As wise person Brené Brown said, "There are no prerequisites for worthiness." The same Universe that created such wonders as Victoria Falls, the Northern Lights, and the Great Barrier Reef brought us you.

Somewhere along your life journey though, people may have tried to convince you otherwise. Hurt people hurt people. But, and I cannot stress this enough, they lied. They were wrong. Their words and actions have no relation to the magic that is you. Wise person Brené Brown also had this to say: "If we want to live and love with our whole hearts, and if we want to engage with the world from a place of worthiness, we have to talk about the things that get in the way—especially shame, fear, and vulnerability."

You've been carrying those heavy weights around for far too long. It's time to let them go and begin again. It's never too late for a fresh start, because we need you in all your perfect imperfection. And you need you in all your glory to not just survive, but to enjoy this one precious life you've been given. As a wise anonymous person said, "The beauty of life is, while we cannot undo what is done, we can see it, understand it, learn from it, and change so that every new moment is spent not in regret, guilt, fear, or anger, but in wisdom, understanding, and love."

As always, may we go in peace and gratitude, may we always know our true worth, and may the Universe shower us with blessings.

Amen.

Today's hymn is *Greatest Love of All* by Whitney Houston. Let us grab our pretend microphone and belt it out together as we sing.

What weight can you let go of this week that would lead you to greater feelings of self-worth?

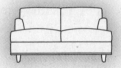

BLESSINGS IN DISGUISE

Hello again, most awesome and amiable Angels. Gather close as we figuratively join hands and join hearts to come together for a little while of quiet reflection.

I come to you today to talk about curses—specifically those that turned out to be blessings in disguise. Mine took the form of a little blond Tasmanian devil of a child.

For many years, I was a fourth-grade teacher. One year, I had recess duty supervising the third-grade playground. For those of you who view elementary school through the soft-focus lens of a Hallmark movie, I must disabuse you of that notion. Every day when the release bell rang at 9:40 A.M., about 300 tiny tikes would reenact the storming of the beaches at Normandy.

Among those mildly rabid squirrels hell-bent on getting to the basketball courts first, one stood out. His long hair flying behind him, he always seemed to leave a trail of disruption and upset tattlers in his wake. I knew the moment I laid eyes on him, the way you know that an earthquake has indeed knocked your house off its foundation, that he was destined to be in my class the following year.

And so, I began a preemptive strike mission to try to calm the beast. I hoped if I could at least build a relationship with this wild child, it might make my last year heading into retirement a little easier. I made a point to chat with him on the playground. His mom taught an after-school program in my classroom, and he would tag along. One day, I started finding notes from him on my desk with the answer to our geography quizzes. Each time, I'd respond by sending a little prize to him in care of his teacher.

Flash forward to the following August. We were a large school of about 1,100 students, and there were nine fourth-grade classes alone. But there was his name on my roster. So, that year, my mission continued. I made him a team leader and gave him little jobs to do. I appreciated his bright and inquisitive mind. I got annoyed with his impulsivity, and I worried that his future teachers might squelch his magic.

Sometimes, people ask me how I get ideas for these sermons. Most of the time, I really don't know—lots of random things inspire me. But one Tuesday, the sermon wrote itself. I was on campus for a meeting, so my students had a sub. I came to the classroom to pick something up at recess, and there were a few of my kiddos outside. As I walked up, my special one read my sweatshirt and said, "Vintage Teacher? That's an understatement!" I jokingly told him that was an F for the day. Our little group joked some more, and then out of nowhere he said, "And that's your hug for the day!" and squeezed me tight. I laughed and told him that now he brought his grade back up.

I realized in that moment that the thing that I dreaded and thought would be a curse, actually turned out to be a blessing. I thought this kid would give me a nervous breakdown by the end of the year, but my class wouldn't have been the same without him, even on the days he blurted out 15 ba-zillion times. Other teachers remarked at how well he was doing. I wish I could've taken all the credit, but he also had some help getting his biochemistry in balance, and he grew up along the way. Okay, so sometimes elementary school is a bit like a Hallmark movie.

Now Dearest, I ask you—is there a small area in your life, that maybe, with a little love and nurturing could be turned around and be a blessing in disguise? Nothing toxic. Just a situation where a change of perspective might make a difference.

As always, may we go in peace and gratitude, may blessings chase us down, and may the Universe shower us with blessings.

Amen.

Today's hymn is *I Can See Clearly Now* by Johnny Nash. Let us sing.

D escribe a situation where you discovered a blessing in disguise.

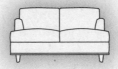

WHY

Hello again, most intelligent and interesting Angels. Gather close as we figuratively join hands and join hearts to come together for a little while of quiet reflection.

I come to you today to talk about our why—why we are here on this third rock from the sun and why we rise to meet each day. Wise person Gail Hyatt said, "People lose their way when they lose their why." It happens to us all—life has a way of knocking the stuffing out of us from time to time, so I think it's important to examine what motivates us now and again.

As wise person Marilynne Robinson said, "There are a thousand reasons to live this life, every one of them sufficient." It can be difficult to see through a fog of depression or anxiety just how surrounded we are by the amazing and awe-inspiring. How about that indoor plumbing? Or coffee, the ocean, stars, hugs, music, our pets, and our people? Every day we get to experience this magnificence, and that ain't nothing. And while we're at it, let's spare a quick minute for some gratitude for those things that make life worth living.

As wise one Marie Curie said, "Life is not easy for any of us. But what of that? We must have perseverance and, above all, confidence in ourselves. We must believe we are gifted for something and that this thing must be obtained." We all have talents that we can tap into to bring our "why" to fruition. For example, many folks would say they are here to care for others—children, significant others, family, and friends, and those less fortunate. Being nurturing, loving, and kind helps us serve this purpose.

Now, Dearest, I applaud your generous and loving heart, but a word of caution to work toward balance. As wise person Lecrae said, "If you live for people's acceptance, you will die from their rejection." So, while serving others is a critical part of our journey, let us also seek a purpose that is just for ourselves. Love yourself enough to figure out what gives you that special spark and grant yourself permission to follow your dreams.

Wise one Saravanan said, "When we born, we gonna die one day. When we lit a candle, it gonna die at the end. When a flower starts to blooming, it gonna be taken anytime. The thing is everything has a end, but it has some reasons. Life is too, live your life with a passion and make your end reasonable." Which just goes to show that wisdom and grammar don't always have to go together.

As always, may we go in peace and gratitude, may we embrace our whys, and may the Universe shower us with blessings.

Amen.

Today's hymn is *Born for This* by the Score. Let us crank it up and sing.

What is your "why"? How did you discover it?

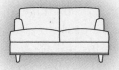

INTUITION

Good morning, most keen and kindhearted Angels. Gather close as we figuratively join hands and join hearts to come together for a little while of quiet reflection.

I want to talk with you today about your intuition—your inner wisdom. We all have that still, small voice inside of us that speaks to us when we are at a crossroads. Sometimes it is when we must make a decision—in the immortal words of The Clash, "Should I stay, or should I go?" Sometimes it is when we are picking up on some sort of negative energy in our surroundings—such as when Chad from Accounting gives you the heebie jeebies, or when you take evasive maneuvers seconds before an errant squirrel runs a suicide mission in front of your car.

As wise woman Shakti Gawain once said, "There is a universal, intelligent life force that exists within everyone and everything. It resides within each one of us as a deep wisdom, an inner knowing. We can access this wonderful source of knowledge and wisdom through our intuition, an inner sense that tells us what feels right and true for us at any given moment."

But how do I access my Spidey Sense, you ask? If you aren't in the habit of listening, it takes a bit of practice. First of all, you must get quiet. Your intuition is not shouty and demanding. It will not yell over your video game or social media posting. Just be present for a minute and listen. We have to engage all of our senses and limit our distractions if we want to hear the call to action.

How will I know if it's working, you ask? My, you have a lot of questions today! Have you ever had a friend ask for relationship advice and you knew instantly what they should do? Or you knew what they really wanted to do but just needed validation? It's when you take the facts and combine them with the feelings that you are well on your way. And when you have come to the decision that is right for you, verily, you will feel a peace about it.

All too often, though, we override this wisdom. We fear looking foolish or causing a scene. It is important to honor the inner voice because it is there to keep you physically and emotionally safe. It is better to be embarrassed than harmed. We need to get in the difficult habit of acting immediately and asking questions later rather than second-guessing ourselves in the moment.

So, I commend you, when next you are presented with a decision, listen for that voice. It's your voice, Dearest, and it is beautiful and wise. As wise and knowing person Alan Alda once said, "At times, you have to leave the city of your comfort and go into the wilderness of your intuition. What you'll discover will be wonderful. What you'll discover is yourself."

As always, may we go in peace and gratitude, may we trust that still small voice, and may the Universe shower us with blessings.

Amen.

Today's hymn is what else? *Intuition* by Jewel.
Let us sing.

D o you consider yourself intuitive? How might you engage your intuition this week?

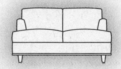

BOOMERANG

Hello again, most stunning and stupendous Angels. Gather close as we figuratively join hands and join hearts to come together for a little while of quiet reflection.

I come to you today to talk about Newton's Third Law. For those of us who last studied physics back in high school, allow me to refresh your memory. The gist of it is that for every action, there is an equal and opposite reaction. Call it karma or kismet or just rewards—there seems to be a boomerang effect going on in the Universe when it comes to the type of energy we send out.

As wise person Sophia Amoruso said, "It is the age-old concept of like attracts like, or the law of attraction. You get back what you put out, so you might as well think positively, focus on visualizing what you want instead of getting distracted by what you don't want, and send the universe your good intentions so that it can send them right back."

Do I have any hard, scientific proof that this is in fact how things work? No, I do not.

I could try to convince you that it is true because I want so badly to believe that there is a force in the Universe that ensures that good people get back what they give out and awful people get back a flaming dumpster of manure. A cosmic justice if you will. But I'm not so naive as to think that is always the case.

Or I could tell you a lot of personal stories where I found this to be the case. Like how, in writing these sermons with the intention to be helpful, I've gotten back so much more in the lovely comments that folks have shared. Or how, when I've offered help to some people who were homeless, I received the most angelic smiles I've ever seen, and my heart was full.

Instead, I'll leave it to one of the brightest minds the world has ever known. Wise person Albert Einstein said, "Everything is energy and that's all there is to it. Match the frequency of the reality that you want and you cannot help but get that reality. It can be no other way. This is not philosophy. This is physics."

If you have not been on the receiving end of the good stuff, Dearest, let's get to the bottom of that right now. First of all, you have to pay attention. Sometimes the good will sneak up on you like a tiny flower peeking out of a crack in the sidewalk. Or the softly spoken compliment that we too easily dismiss. You have to pay attention. It will not always slap you upside the head while you rush through your life staring down at your phone.

Next, you have to make sure that you are not surrounded by a feral pack of takers. Sometimes we get all the goodness and light sucked up by those who would take advantage of us. Be around others who are positive and giving and distance yourself from the rest.

Finally, start small. There is no better way to start than with some random acts of kindness aimed at strangers and loved ones alike. Hold a door, do a favor, donate, volunteer. As wise person Zig Ziglar said, "Life is an echo. What you send out, comes back. What you sow, you reap. What you give, you get. What you see in others, exists in you. Remember, life is an echo. It always gets back to you. So give goodness."

As always, may we go in peace and gratitude, may our good find its way back to us each and every day, and may the Universe shower us with blessings.

Amen.

Today's hymn is *Good Vibrations* by the Beach Boys. Let us grab our surfboards and sing.

D escribe a time when your good came back to you.

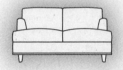

AUTUMN

Hello again, most creative and compassionate Angels. Gather close as we figuratively join hands and join hearts to come together for a little while of quiet reflection.

Grab a pumpkin spice latte, throw on a comfy sweater, and curl up in front of the fire because I come to you today to talk about fall. Ever since I can remember, I've loved this season most of all—maybe it's the cooler temperatures, the smell of woodsmoke in the air, or the vibrant colors of the leaves. Maybe it's, as wise person Lauren DeStefano said, "Fall has always been my favorite season. The time when everything bursts with its last beauty, as if nature had been saving up all year for the grand finale."

Without too much of a stretch, I think that fall has some lovely lessons to teach us. First, as wise person John Burroughs said, "How beautifully leaves grow old. How full of light and color are their last days." Many people dread the passage of time. While I'm discovering some unique challenges on my journey of aging, I feel grateful that I have been given the gift of growing older, which is something that lots of folks have been denied. Wear every scar, every wrinkle, and every gray hair on your head as a badge of honor and courage that you have earned, you gorgeous creature.

And, as a wise anonymous person said, "Autumn shows us how beautiful it is to let things go." What can you let go of today, Dearest? The weight of remorse and regret? The nagging doubts and worries? The toxic relationship? You have been carrying these things on your heart for far too long. It's like an acrobat on the trapeze— you have to release something to take hold of the new. Trust in yourself and take that leap. There's no better time than today.

Maybe it's because I taught for so many years, but fall always feels like the start of the new year for me—new students, planning out new activities, the smell of freshly sharpened pencils. As wise person F. Scott Fitzgerald said, "Life starts all over again when it gets crisp in the fall." Where are you in need of a new beginning? Maybe it's time to finally take that class, go for that promotion, give that dream a second chance. As long as you're breathing, it's never too late. Even if things haven't worked out in the past, the Universe is saying to you, "Begin again."

Finally, wise person Sir Kristian Goldmund Aumann said, "Autumn is the time of picturesque tranquility." That is a stellar reminder to carve out some time to hop off the merry-go-round of life, turn off the electronics, and reconnect with the world—even if it's just for a few moments. Take some deep breaths of the fall air, jump in a pile of leaves, pick some apples, go for a walk, refresh your spirit.

As always, may we go in peace and gratitude, may our fall be filled with comfort and renewal, and may the Universe shower us with blessings.

Amen.

Today's hymn is *September* by Earth, Wind & Fire. Let us throw on some gold lamé and sing.

What do you like best about fall? Share a special seasonal memory that you have.

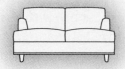

VISION

Hello again, most magical and majestic Angels. Gather close as we figuratively join hands and join hearts to come together for a little while of quiet reflection.

I come to you today to talk to you about vision—specifically where and what we are keeping in our line of sight. To paraphrase the immortal words of Johnny Lee, all too often, we are looking for life in all the wrong places.

Some of us spend far too much time focused on the past. Now, there's nothing wrong with the occasional stroll down memory lane, but Dearest, there is a reason that the rearview mirror is so much smaller than the windshield. As a wise anonymous person said, "Stop looking back. There's nothing there. Your healing, blessings, and miracles are ahead of you, not behind you." So, a brief visit to the Land of What Used to Be is fine, but no setting up camp there, especially in hopes of changing what cannot be changed.

Some of us spend far too much time focused on the future. We are busy worrying about real or imagined tragedies that may befall us. Or we have a line of wishful thinking going on that at some point on the horizon, we will find our happiness. When we lose the weight, when it's time for our vacation, when we get the bills paid off, then we can finally be happy. But worrying never changed an outcome. And as wise person Abdu'l-Bahá said, "If we are not happy and joyous at this season, for what other season shall we wait and for what other time shall we look?"

So where should we be looking? Permit me to offer a couple of suggestions. First, be on the lookout for blessings. So often, they are right in front of us—our family, friends, furry loves, health, food on the table, and a roof over our heads. As wise person Rhonda Byrne said, "Never let a day pass without looking for the good, feeling the good within you, praising, appreciating, blessing, and being grateful. Make it your life commitment and you will stand in utter awe of what happens in your life."

If you're already an accomplished staying-in-the-now blessing detective, then you are ready for the Zen Master level. Time to go big. As wise person Daisaku Ikeda said, "It is important that we have the inner richness to be able to look up at the stars or the moon and compose a poem once in a while. When we open wide our minds and fix our gaze on the universe, we fix our gaze on our own life."

May we all let go of the past, embrace the future while knowing it will take care of itself, and be open to the wonders all around us.

As always, may we go in peace and gratitude, may our vision be clear, and may the Universe shower us with blessings.

Amen.

Today's hymn is *Don't Look Back* by Boston. Let us sing.

W here will you focus your vision this week?

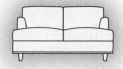

WARRIOR

Hello again, most prized and perfect Angels of Heaven. Gather close as we figuratively join hands and join hearts to come together for a little while of quiet reflection.

I come to you to talk about words—specifically those words that have been used to make us feel small and beaten down. Those words might have come from strangers, but all too often, they came from those who should be using words to lift us up instead—friends, family, teachers, and clergy. As wise person Luis Marques said, "Words are more dangerous than swords and guns. They reach further and hurt deeper."

But those hurtful words could not be further from the truth. We were all born mighty warriors, capable at once of great strength and tenderness, fearlessness and kindness, bravery and loyalty—all beyond measure. Look into your eyes, Dearest. Even if you haven't felt it in a while, all of those fierce qualities still reside within you. As wise woman Cassandra Clare said, "Whatever you are physically . . . male or female, strong or weak, ill or healthy—all those things matter less than what your heart contains. If you have the soul of a warrior, you are a warrior. All those other things, they are the glass that contains the lamp, but you are the light inside."

How do we keep our light burning bright in a world that is constantly trying to put out that flame? First, we can look to the warriors around us—ordinary people who do extraordinary things. The health care workers, the emergency responders, the teachers—there are people in our communities who may not be famous, but they are heroes. Let their stories inspire us to bigger things.

Next, we can start with some small steps. You can tap into your inner superhero and literally save someone's life by donating blood, signing up to be an organ or bone marrow donor, or learning CPR and basic first aid. Or we can volunteer our time and resources to help those in need. We can't do everything, but we can do one thing. As wise person Jana Stanfield said, "I cannot do all the good that the world needs, but the world needs all the good that I can do."

Lastly, but perhaps most importantly, we have to distance ourselves from the toxic ones. Easier said than done, especially when they may live or work with you, I know. Then it is even more imperative that we drown them out with words of our own. As wise one Beryl Nyamwange said, "It matters what you say in your head about what you think in your heart. Be your own encourager." Remind yourself that you are braver than you know and stronger than you think.

As always, may we go in peace and gratitude, may we remember how strong and brave we truly are, and may the Universe shower us with blessings.

Amen.

Today is another double hymn day—*Warrior* by Scandal and *We Are the Champions* performed by Child Prodigy on YouTube. Let us sing it like we mean it.

Describe a time when you were brave. How did it feel?

VOICE

Hello again, most genuine and generous Angels. Gather close as we figuratively join hands and join hearts to come together for a little while of quiet reflection.

I come to you today to talk about our voices. When I was teaching fourth grade, I would often have my students do small-group discussions. As I eavesdropped on their conversations, I noticed that it was often the same children who spoke first and loudly and the same ones who spoke last and softly. Even trying creative ways to mix up who went first seemed to have little impact. It was time to get direct.

So, I shared with these nine-year-olds the results of a study from the *Journal of Language and Social Psychology* that found that men interrupt women an average of 2.1 times over the course of a three-minute conversation. When men talked to men, they interrupted nearly one-third less. The kids were shocked.

And I challenged them, as I'm challenging you today, to self-reflect. If you are the one whose voice is gentle and soft, but often silenced or ignored, then I'm asking you to speak up and speak out. We need your thoughts and ideas—maybe now more than ever. As a wise anonymous person said, "A comfort zone is a beautiful thing, but nothing ever grows there." Here are some handy phrases to help you out:

"Excuse me, I wasn't finished."

"Please don't interrupt."

"I respectfully disagree."

And, Dearest, if you are the one doing the interrupting, it's time to take a step back. It's time to let someone else have the floor. That means taking a breath before speaking. That means not thinking about possible solutions to fix the situation or coming up with what you'll say next. As wise person Elizabeth Laser said, "Don't persuade, defend, or interrupt. Be curious, be conversational, be real. And listen."

Like my students, we will have mixed success. For the most part, they were able to identify when they needed to step forward or step back, and the other students were more than happy to help them figure it out. But they stumbled with moving beyond hearing to really listening as we adults often do. It takes intention and practice.

Our brothers, sisters, and non-binary siblings are raising their voices now. When the time comes, will we step back so that they can be heard? Will we step forward and lend our voice? As Richard Nixon said, "Each moment in history is a fleeting time, precious and unique. But some stand out as moments of beginning, in which courses are set that shape decades or centuries." Which just goes to show that even people who lack a moral compass can still illustrate a point.

As always, may we go in peace and gratitude, may we find our voice and help others to find theirs, and may the Universe shower us with blessings.

Amen.

Today's hymn, inspired by Thelma Mothershed Wair and Elizabeth Eckford of the Little Rock Nine, is *Blackbird* by Paul McCartney. Let us sing.

D o you need to step forward or step back this week? How will you accomplish it?

SPARK

Good morning, most witty and winning Angels. Gather close as we figuratively join hands and join hearts to come together for a little while of quiet reflection.

I come to you today to talk about getting your spark back. For many of us, just surviving can be a major challenge. We have bills to pay, a roof to keep over our heads, food to get on the table. And so, putting one foot in front of the other, we get up, go to work, come home, and do it all over again the next day until life becomes our personal version of *Groundhog Day*. It's not surprising that we lose our zip. But, as wise person Colette Werden said, "It's okay if you lose your spark. Just make sure that when you get back up, you rise as the whole damn fire."

So how do we break out of the routine rut? The first two steps involve invoking the wisdom of children. You'd be hard-pressed to find a child who has lost their innate sparkle. Their main task in life is to learn things, and so they possess a sometimes inordinate amount of curiosity. Ever been besieged by a child asking a string of whys? Then you know what I mean. We need to tap into that natural wonder we tucked away and start asking why again. As wise person Bryant H. McGill said, "Curiosity is one of the great secrets of happiness." Instead of jumping down an endless rabbit hole of cat videos, amusing as they may be, use the power of the Internet to find out why. Why do cats purr? Why do stars twinkle? Why do we dream?

Once upon a time, we were experts at play, as most children are. That's how we learned about the world and how to get along with other people. Little by little, we found more time for work and less time for play. But, as wise person George Bernard Shaw said, "We don't stop playing because we grow old. We grow old because we stop playing." So, turn up the music and sing in the car, have a food fight, swing on the swings.

Another piece of advice comes from wise person Ruth Gordon who said, "Try something new each day. After all, we're given life to find it out. It doesn't last forever." Sometimes new things make us feel awkward. I am guilty of unrealistically wanting to do something perfectly the first time out. So, I joined a bowling league and learned to embrace my 125 average. Step out of your comfort zone and try a new food, learn a new language, take a dance class. See if that doesn't put a little pep in your step.

One of the reasons that we lose our spark may be that we are exhausted by the demands of life. What are we saying yes to and what are we saying no to? Say no to things that steal your joy. Say no to the takers and users. Say no to things that don't sync with what you value. But as wise person Annie Downs said, "Say yes to the situations that stretch you and scare you and ask you to be better than you think you can be."

And, Dearest, if it's your otherwise healthy relationship that has lost its spark? Well, a lot of these suggestions work with partners too. Be silly and play together, try new things, learn something new together. Remember back to the days when you first fell in love—what were the things that endeared them to you? Put the phone away, talk, touch, and appreciate the time that you have been given together. Tomorrow isn't guaranteed.

As always, may we go in peace and gratitude, may we sparkle and twinkle and shine, and may the Universe shower us with blessings.

Amen.

Today's hymn is *Dancing in the Dark* by Bruce Springsteen. Let us sing.

What is one strategy you will try to put some spark in the week ahead?

Part 4: Gifts

EACH DAY
PROVIDES ITS
OWN GIFTS.

— Marcus Aurelius

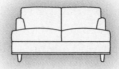

BIRD BY BIRD

Hello again, most bewitching and beguiling Angels. Gather close as we once again figuratively join hands and join hearts to come together for a little while of quiet reflection.

I come to you today to share a story from author Anne Lamott. A friend recently gave me one of her books, and when I turned it over, I found this. Just a blurb on the back of a book, but oh what a blurb! She wrote . . .

> Thirty years ago, my older brother, who was ten years old at the time, was trying to get a report on birds written that he'd had three months to write, which was due the next day. We were out at our family cabin in Bolinas, and he was at the kitchen table close to tears, surrounded by binder paper and pencils and unopened books on birds, immobilized by the hugeness of the task ahead. Then my father sat down beside him, put his arm around my brother's shoulder, and said, "Bird by bird, buddy. Just take it bird by bird."

How many times have we found ourselves in that situation—paralyzed by the task in front of us? It may be due to our own procrastination, but that's a sermon for another day. Many times, life in all its comedic and tragic twists and turns, just presents these mountains to us. Maybe it's personal, like having to relocate your life and belongings or managing the care of a loved one. Maybe it's working to make the world a kinder and better place.

In these times, all we can see is an insurmountable situation. The doubt creeps in and freezes us in place. That's when we have to take a deep breath or 20 and reflect on these wise words from Christina Roberson: "When the week ahead seems overwhelming, focus on the day. If the day at hand is causing you stress, think only of the hour. When the hour seems as if it will last forever, try living in the moment. When you feel you cannot handle the moment, count to 60 and it will be over!"

And we repeat to ourselves, "bird by bird." We don't have to do everything at once. One phone call, one chapter, one petition at a time. As wise one Dr. Martin Luther King Jr. said, "You don't have to see the whole staircase. Just take the first step." And, Dearest, what if we don't know which step is the first? Then just pick one and take it. There is no wrong place to start—it's all about the forward motion overcoming the paralysis. Rest, if you need to, but keep going.

Our fear can be a big part of what holds us in place. Fear of failure or, ironically, fear of success. Fear of falling short, disappointing ourselves and others. No one wants to experience that hurt. But take heart, and may these wise words from Glennon Doyle inspire you: "I see your pain, and it's big. I also see your courage and it's bigger. You can do hard things."

As always, may we go in peace and gratitude, may we take a step in the right direction today, and may the Universe shower us with blessings.

Amen.

Today's hymn is *Rockin' Robin* by Bobby Day. Let us shake a tail feather as we sing.

What is one thing that you can tackle "bird by bird" this week? How will you break it down into doable steps?

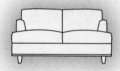

SHINE

Hello again, most impressive and incandescent Angels. Gather close as we figuratively join hands and join hearts to come together for a little while to reflect and refresh.

I come to you today to tell you a story and the lesson I learned from it. I had already been teaching for some time when a new teacher transferred to my school. When I met her, my impressions were that she never had a positive thing to say, and no matter what anecdote, lesson idea, or experience you shared, she'd never fail to go you at least one better. If Debbie Downer and Dwight Schrute had a baby, it would have been her.

One day, I noticed she had done a really cool project with her students. Deciding to act like a proper veteran teacher, I told her it was amazing and asked her if she would show me how to do it with my class. She was more than eager to teach me. But what I really learned that day was that this young woman had developed these personality habits as a defense. Like most of us, all she needed was for someone to acknowledge her and let her know she was doing a good job.

Once I set my judgment aside, I was able to see how bright and funny she was. Instead of avoiding her, I actually began seeking her out to share a laugh or commiserate together. It was one of those aha moments for me on my journey toward judging less and loving more.

I hope today that you will take the opportunity to see past someone's facade to what may lie beneath. You must, of course, protect your own heart, but is there someone you can see in a different light? Is there an opportunity to let them shine? As wise person Elizabeth Lesser said, "Look for a way to lift someone up. And if that's all you do, that's enough."

Since we all have times in our lives when we're uncertain and insecure, we may see a bit of ourselves in that young woman. What then? First of all, don't wait around for someone like me to wake up and have an epiphany. Some of us are a little slow on the uptake. Instead, I think these wise words from Madalyn Beck can point the way. "Start over, my darling. Be brave enough to find the life you want and courageous enough to chase it. Then start over and love yourself the way you were always meant to."

Easier said than done to be sure, but you know what they say about that journey of a thousand miles beginning with a single step. No one can really assure you enough. Deep down you have to know that you know that you are worthy and lovable and perfect in your imperfections. As wise person Buddha said, "You yourself, as much as anybody in the entire universe, deserve your love and affection."

As always, may we go in peace and gratitude, may we look for the best in ourselves and others, and may the Universe shower us with blessings.

Amen.

Today's hymn is a charming reminder of just how special you are: *A, You're Adorable* performed by Chevy on YouTube. Let us sing.

Who can you see in a new light this week?

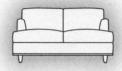

CIRCLE

Hello again, most understanding and uplifting Angels. Gather close as we figuratively join hands and join hearts to come together for a little while of quiet reflection.

I come to you today to talk about the circular nature of life. I saw a trailer for *The Personal History of David Copperfield*. In the clip, an older woman tells David, "You had nothing. Then you had something. Now, you got nothing again. So, it stands to right that you'll have something again." I know that may feel like cold comfort if you are going through a profound loss or disappointment. But I found it rather reassuring. As an anonymous wise person said, "They say all good things come to an end, but we seem to forget that all bad things do, too."

As I dug a little deeper, I found this quote by wise person Chris Murray. He said, "The only time you have is the where and when of right now. There will always be good times, bad times, hard times, and complete disasters. However, there is no other option but to be where you are, when you are. That is a universal truth for everyone. The important thing is how you respond, what you decide to do, and when you decide to do it."

So, how will we respond when the road gets rough? It may help to get some perspective on yourself and the problem. As wise person Joyce Marter said, "You are not your problems or your crisis. You are not your divorce, your illness, your trauma, or your bank account. Your true self is that deeper entity within that is perfectly whole and well no matter what you are experiencing." So instead of maximizing your problem and minimizing yourself, we have to do the opposite. Take a closer look at that situation. Is it truly a catastrophe, a mild disaster, or an inconvenience? One way to determine that is to ask yourself if money can fix it. Now, money may be tight, but money can repair a car, but it can't cure cancer or bring someone back to life.

Then, what will you do? First of all, take good care of yourself—including limiting your time with toxic folks. Acknowledge and feel your feelings. Talk them through with a trusted friend or licensed professional. Then make a plan to act. Decide what you can control and what you can't. Gather the information and resources and ask for help if you need it. As wise person Benjamin Disraeli said, "Action may not always bring happiness, but there is no happiness without action." Way to keep it real, Ben.

Finally, when will we move forward? We may feel inclined to procrastinate, especially when life has knocked us to the ground. Completely understandable, but not ultimately in our best interest. As wise person Kevin Ngo said, "If you don't make the time to work on creating the life you want, you're eventually going to be forced to spend a lot of time dealing with a life you don't want."

So, Dearest, as a wise anonymous person said, "Life is a circle of happiness, sadness, hard times, and good times. If you are going through hard times, have faith that good times are on the way." You've survived 100 percent of your worst days so far. You are tougher than you think and braver than you know. You've got this.

As always, may we go in peace and gratitude, may our troubles be few and our burdens be light, and may the Universe shower us with blessings.

Amen.

Today's hymn is *The Bug* by Mary Chapin Carpenter. Let us sing.

Describe a time in your life where you came through a bad time and into a good one.

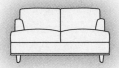

RESILIENCE

Good morning, most treasured and tremendous Angels. Gather close as we figuratively join hands and join hearts to come together for a little while of quiet reflection.

I come to talk to you today about bouncing back. None of us gets through this life without experiencing things that shake us to our core and leave us feeling broken. And while there will be a time for mourning for what we feel should have been, we can bounce back and walk into a bright future. As wise person Maya Angelou said, "I can be changed by what happens to me. But I refuse to be reduced by it."

I know, I know. What doesn't kill you gives you a lot of unhealthy coping mechanisms and a really dark sense of humor. But let me tell you about palm trees. They are one of the most resilient creations on earth. They can be bent to a near-horizontal position in a hurricane. After the storm, while other trees are uprooted and destroyed, palm trees bounce back. Not only do they return to their upright position, but they are actually stronger for having been through the experience. The same resilience is on the inside of you, Dearest.

How can we strengthen our resilience? First, it is important to build connections—through friends and family, support groups of people who have been through the same experience, or talking to a mental health professional. As wise person Kelly Clarkson said, "My friends and family are my support system. They tell me what I need to hear, not what I want to hear and they are there for me in the good and the bad times. Without them I have no idea where I would be and I know that their love for me is what's keeping my head above the water."

Second, although I am not personally a big fan of change, we have no choice but to accept it. As wise person Bob Goff said, "Embrace uncertainty. Some of the most beautiful chapters in our lives won't have titles until much later."

Next, try to enjoy a good laugh. You know—one of those deep baby belly laughs. Studies have shown that laughter releases endorphins and generally helps with better mental health. It's hard when all we want to do is cry, but try to find a movie, a cat video, a meme—anything that will bring on a giggle. As a wise anonymous person said, "Laughter is like a windshield wiper—it doesn't stop the rain, but it allows us to keep going."

And, lastly, as I always admonish, take good care of yourself. Eat fresh foods, drink plenty of water, get enough sleep, and go for a walk. The smallest of upsets can knock you to your knees when you're overtired and have low blood sugar. As this wise person said, "It all begins with you. If you do not care for yourself, you will not be strong enough to take care of anything in life." Which just goes to show that sometimes great wisdom comes from anonymous sources.

As always, may we go in peace and gratitude, may we easily find our inner strength, and may the Universe shower us with blessings.

Amen.

Today is double hymn day! *Stronger* by Kelly Clarkson and *Some Days You Gotta Dance* by the Chicks. Let us sing.

What is one thing you can do to strengthen your resilience this week?

STEADY

Hello again, most amusing and appreciated Angels. Gather close as we figuratively join hands and join hearts to come together for a little while of quiet reflection.

I come to you today to talk to you about staying steady, even when things seem to be falling apart around you. In those times, we can lose our sense of balance and certainty in the world.

I read a story in a longer piece by former reporter and surprisingly poetic soul, Dan Rather, that inspired me. He wrote, "In my early years, I was stricken with rheumatic fever. I can remember hearing my mother crying when she thought she was beyond earshot. I sometimes whimpered at the injustice of my fate, and my father would come into my room to stand over me, lovingly but firmly. 'Steady, Danny,' he would say. 'Steady.' The words were clear and deliberate, and they were soothing."

Those words have become a sort of a mantra to me lately, and I too find them to be soothing. But on those days when we are just about to well and truly lose our er, stuff, what can we do beyond rocking in a corner and saying this word over and over to ourselves?

The first step is in maintaining your routines. This is much easier said than done in times of upheaval in our lives. Now, there's nothing wrong with having a few pajama/binge watch/junk food days in a row as we try to adjust. But once we get that out of our systems, it's time to wipe away the Cheeto dust and reinstate old and create new routines. As wise person Peggy Noonan said, "Part of courage is simple consistency." So, practice those self-care habits, get dressed, make your bed, engage with other people, take a shower—at least most days of the week.

Next, get a clear and honest perspective on what you can and cannot control. As wise person Judith Orloff said, "Being a control freak makes us tense, stressed out, and unpleasant to be with." Guilty as charged. I saw a wonderful graphic that helped me gain some perspective though. Things about this situation that I can't control and therefore must let go of include: predicting what will happen or how long this situation will last or how others react. But things I can control and therefore will focus on include: my kindness and grace, finding fun things to do, turning off the news, and my positive attitude.

Lastly, Dearest, I think it is important for our spirits to take this opportunity to step off the merry-go-round and stop watching our lives go by in a whirlwind. As wise person Doko said, "Just slow down. Slow down your speech. Slow down your breathing. Slow down your walking. Slow down your eating. And let this slower, steadier pace perfume your mind. Just slow down . . ." Maybe it's time to lose the frantic, frenetic rushing about once and for all and take time to savor our lives.

As always, may we go in peace and gratitude, may we find our equilibrium in uncertain times, and may the Universe shower us with blessings.

Amen.

Today's hymn is *Steady* by For King and Country.
Let us sing.

Think about an uncomfortable situation in your life. List things that are out of your control and in your control.

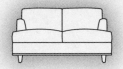

"FAMILY"

Hello again, most respected and resplendent Angels. Gather close as we figuratively join hands and join hearts to come together for a little while of quiet reflection.

I come to you today to talk about your clan—those folks who, through blood or deep friendship, have become family. Our brother from another mother. Our sister from another mister. Our sib from another crib. Those we are lucky enough to be together with on this third rock from the sun at the same time. As wise person Dave Willis said . . . "'Family' isn't defined only by last names or by blood; it's defined by commitment and by love. It means showing up when they need it most. It means having each other's backs. It means choosing to love each other even on those days when you struggle to like each other. It means never giving up on each other."

When my eldest nephew was a toddler, he strode into a family gathering and announced, "Where's my people?" At two, he knew beyond a shadow of a doubt that he was part of our crazy, accepting, loyal, loving tribe. And, as I was clearing out and cleaning up in the process of downsizing, I've been blessed to be reminded of who my people are.

True confession—I am an unapologetic, sentimental fool. I've saved every letter, note, and card I've ever received for the past 30 or more years. I've procrastinated dealing with the boxes of mementos, dreading a melancholy stroll down memory lane. I knew many of these were the last pieces of evidence of those who were no longer in my life because they had passed, had left, or had simply faded off in a different direction. But, instead of feeling entirely sad, I felt embraced and surrounded by their love and friendship. The caring and pride and concern there in black and white reminded my spirit again—I am a beloved daughter, sister, aunt, teacher, friend.

Now, I don't recommend pack-ratting away everything like I did. But, y'all! We used to write letters! Now we text. We let Hallmark do the heavy lifting and barely scribble a signature on the bottom of a card a couple of times a year. We used to print our pictures out! Now, they sit in a cloud in the ether. I know we're busy. Are we truly busier than folks back in the day? Take some time to put in writing how you feel. One day, someone may look back on our words and know they were loved. And stop hiding behind the camera and be in the picture—years from now, the extra fluffiness, lack of makeup, or bad hair day will not matter one bit.

And Dearest, if you are feeling that you are adrift without a clan today, know that you are loved and valued. As children, all we had to do was ask another kid if they wanted to play to make friends. I guarantee that will create an awkward pause if you try that now with another adult. It's not easy, but I'm sending a hug along with a gentle nudge to look around and see where your people are. Some of them are on the interwebs. There is an interesting lid for every quirky pot. Some of them live in your neighborhood, work in your building, shop at the same stores. They are looking for you too, and they need your smile, your warmth, and your caring.

As always, may we go in peace and gratitude, may we love one another, and may the Universe shower us with blessings.

Amen.

Today's hymn is *Friends in Low Places* by Garth Brooks on YouTube. Let us sing it loud and proud.

Who are the members of your clan that you are most grateful for?

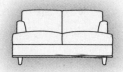

APPRECIATION

Hello again, most likable and lively Angels. Gather close as we figuratively join hands and join hearts to come together for a little while of quiet reflection.

I come to you today to talk about appreciation—particularly about the importance of expressing it to those in our lives. All too often, we let the opportunity to say thank you pass us by. We're busy. Or it might be awkward. Or we think that if we told the person once seven years ago, they should know how we feel. No, Dearest. Those are just excuses, not reasons. As wise person Brigitte Nobel said, "Never fail to appreciate someone who cares for you. Just because they're always in your life to help in some way, never fail to give thanks or recognition. To value someone or something too lightly is a risk no one should take."

The best place to start may be close to home—with our family and friends. It's easy to take those loved ones for granted because they are there day in and day out. We may not even notice those small kindnesses anymore—the cup of coffee we're handed, the pat on the back, the pep talks. But what would our life be like without them? As wise person Ralph Marston said, "Make it a habit to tell people thank you. To express your appreciation, sincerely and without the expectation of anything in return. Truly appreciate those around you, and soon you'll find many others around you. Truly appreciate life, and you find that you have more of it."

Next, let us look around us for those we run into as we move through our days—our co-workers, the waitstaff, the mail carrier, or the stranger who holds the door for us. If it's been a while since you showed them some love, there's no time like the present. If the words don't come easily, just start with thank you. Thank you for your help. Thank you for always starting my day off right. It may seem like a small thing, but as wise person Randy Pausch reminds us, "Showing gratitude is one of the simplest, yet most powerful things humans can do for one another."

And now we come to what may be the trickiest of all— expressing appreciation for ourselves. What is it about yourself that you are thankful for? Your ability to put people at ease? To laugh at your foibles? To work hard and see a project through to completion? Your kind and caring heart? As wise person Robert Holden said, "No amount of self-improvement can make up for any lack of self-acceptance." So when we're doling out the gratitude, let's not be stingy with ourselves.

As we go about our business in the week ahead, let's be on the lookout for moments when we can give thanks to the good folks around us. As wise person Margaret Cousins said, "Appreciation can make a day, even change a life. Your willingness to put it into words is all that is necessary."

As always, may we go in peace and gratitude, may we never leave a kind word unsaid, and may the Universe shower us with blessings.

Amen.

Today's hymn is *Shower the People* by James Taylor. Let us sing.

Who will you thank this week? How will you show yourself some love?

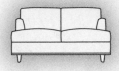

STORIES

Hello again, most fascinating and friendly Angels. Gather close as we figuratively join hands and join hearts to come together for a little while of quiet reflection.

I come to you today to talk about our stories. I was reading an article by Emil Anton on the ways we measure our success. If you ask folks how they know if they've made it, they often respond with wealth or fame. Of course, we all need money to survive, and being known for something special would be nice. But Anton suggests that it's more about having lived a life filled with stories. As a wise anonymous person said, "Fill your life with adventures, not things. Have stories to tell, not stuff to show."

As children, we have so many stories to share. Just ask any teacher who has tried to have a guided discussion and watched it run right off the rails. (Although, honestly, those were some of my favorite times—kids are hella smart and funny.) But, as adults, we seem to lose some of this magical power. Maybe we become less aware or more self-conscious. But, as the fabulous and wise Viola Davis said, "We are all worthy of telling our stories and having them heard. We all need to be seen and honored in the same way we need to breathe."

It got me to thinking about a story that my nieces, nephews, and students asked me to tell again and again— The Story of How I Got Locked in School . . .

For some reason that day, the custodial staff had finished early, so I ended up being the last person on campus. I gathered up my stuff and headed toward the parking lot only to discover that the gate was padlocked. And all the other points of access were locked too. As I stood in the courtyard, I realized I was trapped.

In those days, our classroom phones only called the office and cell phones were still a ways off. I was forced to channel my inner MacGyver, so I started looking around for what I could use. Because if I couldn't go through, I'd have to go over. There was a short step ladder of sorts, and I remembered I had some speaker wire in my room. So, I fashioned a stirrup, tied it to the gate, and hoisted myself up on the roof. In my version of the story, this was done very athletically and gracefully.

One thing you should know is that I'm afraid of heights. So, while I was elated to find myself halfway there, I was pretty terrified of falling off the roof. I surveyed my landing options. A rust-covered chain link structure where I was certain to contract lockjaw and perhaps be impaled. Or a dumpster that was undoubtedly filled with all manner of disgusting school lunch remains where I might crash land into that mess or bounce off the lid and onto the ground.

Just as I was about to give in to despair, I noticed one of my students on the sidewalk across the street. I yelled, "April!" at the top of my lungs, and I swear she looked straight up to the sky as if the voice of God were calling to her from above.

I finally was able to get her attention and asked if her family had a ladder. Her dad brought one over, and I was able to climb down to safety with only slight damage to my dignity. That experience earned me a master school key should I ever find myself in that situation again.

As you can see, the stories don't have to be impressive to be worth sharing. Just take some time to notice the little absurdities or curiosities around you. As wise person Lisa Cron writes in her book *Wired for Story*, "Story, as it turns out, was crucial to our evolution—more so than opposable thumbs. Opposable thumbs let us hang on; story told us what to hang on to."

As always, may we go in peace and gratitude, may abundant health and wellness surround us all, may we find limitless stories to share, may we record the stories of our elders, and may the Universe shower us with blessings.

Amen.

Today's hymn is *Story of My Life* by One Direction. Let us sing.

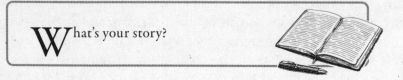

What's your story?

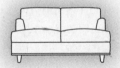

CLOSED DOORS

Hello again, most able and agile Angels. Gather close as we figuratively join hands and join hearts to come together for a little while of quiet reflection.

I come to you today to talk about doors—specifically, those that are metaphorically and, all too often, unceremoniously closed in our faces. As we grieve the end of a relationship or the rug being yanked out from under us in some other way, we are offered what, at the time, seems to be cold comfort—that another door, a better door will be opened soon.

More times than I would like to admit, despite being admonished not to, I have indeed let the door hit me where the good Lord split me. And upon being knocked to the ground by the impact, I have gaped open-mouthed like a fish out of water gasping, for air. It wasn't pretty, and the very last thing that I wanted to hear was that it was necessary for me to experience this pain in order to get to some unspecified better place. Fists were shaken in righteous indignation, and expletives were most certainly uttered.

Eventually, ever the optimist, I would get up, brush myself off, and channel my inner Charlie Brown in search of a Lucy waiting to swipe a football out from under me. And in the hindsight of honest reflection, I can somewhat grudgingly admit that because of those closed doors, my life went in a different and yes, better direction.

Then, I had a bit of an epiphany. I turned in my retirement paperwork to the state agency and my letter of resignation to the school district. The next day, before my dry erase pens were even cold, my resignation letter had been accepted, and in a few months, I was to be on my way out. I blinked a few times, as you do when something you have been planning for a long time "instantly" happens. And then I realized that I had closed a door myself on a 32-year teaching career and was indeed on my way to that unspecified better.

So, if the difference is in being the closer versus being the closee, then Dearest, it must be a matter of gently but honestly reminding ourselves that we must be more mature than that. As wise person Alexander Graham Bell said, "When one door closes, another one opens; but we often look so long and so regretfully at the closed door that we do not see that one that has opened for us."

No one gets their way 100 percent of the time, and if we can accept that as not necessarily being a bad thing, then those words may actually have the power to give us the comfort that we need. Like these from G. K. Gokulkrishnan . . .

When the doors are closing one by one, two probabilities are there. They didn't deserve you or they didn't need you. If you know who you are and what you can do, then just don't care and move on. Because attitude makes the lion the king of the jungle. Create a good present. That will make your past better on the next day. And this will give you the will to make your best future.

Ah, then the key is to shift our perspective. Easier said than done, I know. As wise person Andy Rooney explained, "The closing of a door can bring blessed privacy and comfort—the opening, terror. Conversely, the closing of a door can be a sad and final thing—the opening a wonderfully joyous moment." You don't have to deal with all the closed doors from your past at once but consider taking some baby steps toward reconciliation today.

As always, may we go in peace and gratitude, may we experience countless fabulous new beginnings, and may the Universe shower us with blessings.

Amen.

Today's hymn is *Better Days* by the Goo Goo Dolls.

Describe a time when a closed door led you to a better place.

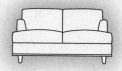

NEVER SURRENDER

Hello again, most superb and sumptuous Angels. Gather close as we figuratively join hands and join hearts to come together for a little while of quiet reflection.

Many of us carry heaviness in our hearts and feelings of despair. Sometimes it seems that the world is a swirling mass of upheaval and dysfunction, hell-bent on destroying the beautiful planet we call home. Some of us are walking difficult personal paths as well, dealing with trauma and loss. It's easy to lose faith that things will ever return to normal or that we will find our way again.

And while we must sometimes go with the twists and turns of life, we must never give up or give in, Dearest. As wise person J. Michael Straczynski said, "There is a greater darkness than the one we fight. It is the darkness of the soul that has lost its way. The war we fight is not against powers and principalities; it is against chaos and despair. Greater than the death of flesh is the death of hope, the death of dreams. Against this peril, we can never surrender."

So, what can we do when we feel that all hope is lost, and we want nothing more than to lie down and quit the fight? First, we must learn when to step off the roller coaster of life and take a breather. Turn off the news, take a break from social media, and go enjoy something or someone you love. As wise person Ralph Marston said, "Rest when you're weary. Refresh and renew yourself, your body, your mind, your spirit. Then get back to work."

Second, we must learn to lean on others. Wise person Michael Moore tells a powerful story of his experience in choir . . .

> Sometimes in band or choir, music requires players or singers to hold a note longer than they actually can hold a note. In those cases, we were taught to mindfully stagger when we took a breath, so the sound appeared uninterrupted. Everyone got to breathe, and the music stayed strong and vibrant . . . Let's remember music. Take a breath. The rest of the chorus will sing. The rest of the band will play. Rejoin so others can breathe. Together, we can sustain a very long, beautiful song for a very, very long time. You don't have to do it all, but you must add your voice to the song.

Lastly, we must tap into our sense of humor and our often-underestimated strength. To paraphrase an anonymous wise person, "When life knocks you down, calmly get back up, smile, and very politely say, 'You hit like a little punk-ass bitch.'"

I have hope, dear Angels, that things will get better, but this will only happen if we stay strong, keep the faith, and hang tough. I leave you with these last words of wisdom from Harriet Beecher Stowe: "Never give up, for that is just the place and time that the tide will turn."

As always, may we go in peace and gratitude, keep fighting the good fight, may we never lose hope, and may the Universe shower us with blessings.

Amen.

Today's hymn is *Never Surrender* by Corey Hart. Let us belt it out as we sing.

Describe a time when you almost gave up but kept on going instead.

THE BLUES

Hello again, most astute and alluring Angels. Gather close as we figuratively join hands and join hearts to come together for a little while of quiet reflection.

I come to you today to talk about the blues. Not the major days of grief and grieving. Just the run-of-the-mill, rainy days and Mondays variety. It happens to us all from time to time. You wake up a little headachy and grumpy. You hit a few minor snags in the road. And next thing you know, you're right in the middle of your very own personal funk. As wise and not particularly uplifting person Domhnall Gleeson said, "Life is difficult for everyone; everyone has bad days. Everyone has trouble in their life, because it doesn't matter how rich you are—sickness and trouble and worry and love, these things will mess with you at every level of life."

But it is a small comfort, I think, to know that we've all been there. And there are times when we just need to acknowledge the blahs and throw ourselves a pity party. Dig out those ratty elastic waist "pants" or tatty old robe, grab your comfort food of choice, and crank up some Adele. But, just a little wallowing—otherwise we run the risk of setting up camp in the Land of Woe is Me. It's good for short visits, but no place to live.

Because, after all, Dearest, as a wise anonymous someone said, "A bad day never equates to a bad life. Feel better as there are days on which you will be victorious. You
might have lost a battle, but you will win the war."

So, scrape the last bit of ice cream out of the carton
and then take a few baby steps forward. I think we can all
use a reminder from time to time for some tried and true
pick-me-ups: Weather permitting, go for a walk or get some
fresh air. Hydrate. Eat some fresh food. Get some sleep. Take
a shower and wash it all down the drain. It's good to feed
your mind and spirit, too. Put on a funny movie, read a
good book, call on a nontoxic loved one, crank up some
tunes. Bad days are more likely to happen when our tanks
are running low, so make sure to recharge.

If all else fails, remember that, in fact, tomorrow is
another day. As the wise and lyric Ralph Waldo Emerson
said . . .

> Finish every day and be done with it.
>
> You have done what you could;
>
> some blunders and absurdities
>
> no doubt crept in;
>
> forget them as soon as you can.
>
> Tomorrow is a new day;
>
> you shall begin it serenely
>
> and with too high a spirit
>
> to be cumbered
>
> with your old nonsense.

So, let us relegate those bad days to the rearview mirror and remind ourselves that while not every day may be
all puppies and rainbows, some of our best days haven't
even happened yet.

As always, may we go in peace and gratitude, may we find peace on the bad days and look ahead to the good, and may the Universe shower us with blessings.

Amen.

Today's hymn is *Better When I'm Dancing* written by Meghan Trainor and performed by the One Voice Children's Choir. Let us shake our booties as we sing.

What have you found works best to pull yourself out of the blues? Is there a new strategy you might try this week?

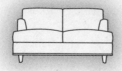

PRICELESS

Hello again, most deep and dazzling Angels. Gather close as we figuratively join hands and join hearts to come together for a little while of quiet reflection.

I come to you today with a question. Do you know your true value? It seems as though many of us struggle to embrace the miracle that we are. We may have been beaten down by circumstances beyond our control to the point where we no longer remember that we are the most wondrous creation of the Universe. It may be hard to believe on some, most, or all days, but it is true, Dearest.

From a purely monetary perspective alone, your body is worth over $45 million, according to Patrick Di Justo in an article for *Wired*. He determined that your DNA, that genetic code that makes you uniquely you—wrinkles, scars, flab, and all—alone is worth about $9 million. You ain't chump change, baby!

But more importantly, you contain within that perfectly flawed body something that's priceless—your beautiful spirit. Your crooked but nevertheless sweet smile that can brighten the day of a stranger. Your tender touch that can comfort a friend. Your corny sense of humor that gives us a laugh. Like ripples in a pond, you have no idea how many lives you have impacted. Go watch or rewatch *It's a Wonderful Life*, for crying out loud. Go. Now. I'll wait . . .

So then, how do we reclaim our value? First of all, you have to throw your shoulders back, hold your head high, stand tall, and walk around like you are the freaking Queen of England. Own every room you walk into. Blast some runway music and strut around your house if you need to practice that confidence. (I'm partial to *The Look* by Roxette myself, but to each their own.) Remind yourself of these words of wise person Sharon Salzberg, "You yourself, as much as anybody in the entire universe, deserve your love and affection."

And now, for some of us, the hardest part of all. We come across situations every day where we have to remind others of our value. Whether it's a bitchy co-worker, a toxic family member, or an emotionally distant lover, we have to draw a line in the sand about what we will and will not tolerate. And we need to know when to walk away. Believe me, Dearest, I know that the hardest thing is to love someone who, for whatever reason, is incapable of loving you the way you want to be loved. As heartbreaking as it may be, you have to let them go. As wise person Robin Williams said, "I used to think the worst thing was to end up alone. It's not. The worst thing in life is to end up with people who make you feel alone."

As always, may we go in peace and gratitude, may we know our immeasurable value down deep in our soul, and may the Universe shower us with blessings.

Amen.

Today's hymn is *Message to Myself* by Melissa Etheridge. Let us sing.

What do you value most about yourself? What do you think others value about you?

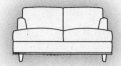

CLOSURE

Hello again, most positive and priceless Angels. Gather close as we figuratively join hands and join hearts to come together for a little while of quiet reflection.

I come to you today to talk about closure—that often-elusive bookend to the conclusion of a relationship, injury, or other loss. For those who have achieved some measure of closure in these situations, a tip of the hat to you. But for many of us, as wise person David Kessler said, "In grief, there is no stage called closure."

I think that when we seek closure, what we are really seeking is an acknowledgment, an apology, an answer to so many whys. We want to understand and be understood. We want justice. But these are things that we have no control over. We can speak our truth, but we can't make someone own up, make amends, or stop them from leaving. As many of us know, that can be a hard and painful pill to swallow.

The good news is that closure doesn't really have to involve anyone else. That's good news because, let's face it Dearest, the other person's response, well-intentioned though it may be, probably isn't going to give us what we really want. To stop hurting. To let go. To feel ready to move on. As wise person John Kim said, "Closure is an inner-self journey. It doesn't require the other person. It requires you to find peace on your own. And the way you do that is on you. It's not contingent on someone else giving you something. And like any journey, it's not a straight line. It's wild and messy. Up and down and sideways and not a one-size-fits-all."

So, where to start? First, allow yourself time to grieve. Don't allow people to tell you to just get over it. But let your grieving be for a season, not for a lifetime. As wise person Leo Tolstoy said, "Only people who are capable of loving strongly can also suffer great sorrow, but this same necessity of loving serves to counteract their grief and heals them."

Gather those people and things that make you feel strong and happy. As wise person Jim Rohn said, "Happiness is not something you postpone for the future; it is something you design for the present." So, reach out to friends and family, pick up a new hobby or one you set aside, plan a visit to your favorite place. Immerse yourself in the positive.

Of course, I'm going to take this opportunity to advocate for taking good care of yourself. When we feel bad, we often overindulge in things that make us feel better for a minute. That can help comfort us and get us over a rough patch. But ultimately, we need to stay hydrated, eat fresh foods, go for walks, and get enough sleep if we're going to tap into our inner strength.

Then, depending on the situation, the best thing we can do may be to forgive ourselves. Easier said than done for sure. We have to remind ourselves that, given what we knew at the time, we did the best we could do. It's time to chalk it up to experience and let it go.

As wise person Dr. Abigail Brenner said, "Closure means finality; a letting go of what once was. Finding closure implies a complete acceptance of what has happened and an honoring of the transition away from what's finished to something new." May those of us who seek closure find it today.

As always, may we go in peace and gratitude, may that weight we've been carrying be lifted, and may the Universe shower us with blessings and humor.

Amen.

Today is another double hymn day. If you're feeling a bit nostalgic, then go with *Bruises* by Train. If you're in need of an anthem to blast, go with *Good as Hell* by Lizzo. Let us sing.

> Describe your experience with closure. How will you celebrate the closing of this year?

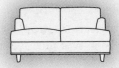

A FINAL WORD

While these sermons are meant to help create connections, they are no substitute for person-to-person bonding. If I might offer up a suggestion—find some like-minded people and read this book together. Discuss your journal entries, which sermon spoke to you the most, what you discovered about yourself, what memories the songs evoked, or anything else your group would like to explore. We are always stronger together.

Thank you for joining me on this yearlong journey. Along the way, I hope you've gained some new insights and been inspired. But, most of all, I hope your belief in yourself and how unique, awesome, and generally butt-kicking you really are has been confirmed and strengthened. The Universe is a better place for having you in it.

You are needed, loved, and cherished, Dearest, and nothing and no one can ever change that.

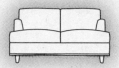

ACKNOWLEDGMENTS

I've taken nearly 60 trips around the sun and have been blessed in every revolution to come across people who, for better or worse, but usually better, have made me the person that I am today. So, to everyone I've known— to those who stayed, those who passed, and those who left, I offer up a heaping heartful of gratitude.

Most especially, I want to thank my family—my parents, Bud and Marilyn, who taught me the importance of education and judging people on the content of the character above all else; my brothers, Brian, Craig, and Matthew, who are a continual source of support and are the funniest people I've ever met. Without them, I wouldn't have my wonderful sisters-in-law Kathy, Jeanine, and Stephanie and my super amazing and incredible nieces and nephews Brandon, Maya, Nathaniel, Madeleine, Cooper, and Gracie. Love you all to the moon and back. And to all my aunts, uncles, and cousins—thank you for being part of my loving tribe, too.

I've been graced to have the most wonderful friends that grew into family. To my sibs from other cribs, thank you for decades of love and laughter as we took our first steps toward adulthood. I look forward to aging gracefully with you all—Kathy Nall, Margaret O'Connell, Mary Ann

Driver, Jon Porterfield, Dave Rees, Kathy Williams, Karen Hughes, Mary Conroy, and Jeff Rubin and their fabulous spouses who patiently tolerate our frequent strolls down memory lane.

I've also been fortunate to have co-workers who turned into family. Shout out to the Fremont folks—the E.M. Grimmer Bears and the Warm Springs Wolves! In particular, my dearest work husband and mentor Fred Turner, who introduced me to the fabulous Shirley McDonald and Anthony Hampton. To Janelle Herrington, Dannie Stafford, Andrea Thornton, Dan Kurtz, Romina Papa, Danielle Girard, Desiree Burbank, Diana Ramirez, Jason Zelt, Heather Driscoll, and Hilary Roberts—your professional and personal support has been invaluable.

And to the most lovely ladies who've worked hard for so long to keep my hair and nails tamed and the knots in my back under control, I'm so pleased to be not only your client, but truly your friend—Karlene Vincenzi, Thuy Ho, and Lupe Higares—you are the very best!

To the city of Astoria, Oregon, the place where my musings became this book. Thank you for all the rainy, watery inspiration. To the wonderful folks I met there— Maya, Bonnie, Doug, Harris, and Liz—thank you for making this California girl feel at home. And sending love to my favorite tree by the river.

I'd also like to thank those who inspired me as a person and a writer. To Louise Hay who taught me about the critical connection between mind and body and who gave me the building blocks that I needed for my spiritual journey. To Pastor Joel Osteen who helped me realize that God was so much more about love than punishment. Thank you for giving me my faith back. And to Anne Lamott whose writings are my favorite sermons. Thank you for reminding me that grace always bats last.

To all the good angels on the Heaven Facebook page—I cannot thank you enough for all the encouragement you've given over the years. Your comments will always be in my heart. This book simply wouldn't have happened without you. To Heaven's founder whoever He or She may be, thank you for allowing me a little corner of your holy space to do my thing. And to those who've visited my Facebook page or blog, you are all greatly appreciated.

To the folks at Hay House who gave me the opportunity of a lifetime and took a chance on a first-time, unknown author. Sincerest thanks to Reid Tracy and Kelly Notaras for your teaching sessions; to my editor Melody Guy for polishing my work while keeping my voice on the page; and to all the "backstage" staff who made publishing this book a reality.

To you, Dearest reader, who took a chance on this book. I am humbled and filled with gratitude.

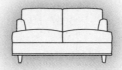

ABOUT THE AUTHOR

Cindy Gentry is a native of Sacramento, California, and has lived in several lovely Northern California cities (plus a few that weren't so great, to be honest). After graduating with a degree in Human Development, minors in English and Education, and receiving her credential from the University of California at Davis, she spent 32 years teaching, mentoring, writing grants, and coordinating peer education and homeless student services. She was twice nominated for Teacher of the Year.

A few years ago, she became an ordained minister with the Universal Life Church, joining fellow clerical alumni such as Sir Paul McCartney, Stephen Colbert, and Lady Gaga, and began posting weekly encouragement, humor, and inspiration posts on a private Facebook group page. Her readers urged her to compile these sermons into an interactive yearlong readers' journey and so her first book, *Sermons on the Couch*, was born.

To learn more about Cindy and her work, visit her website at: www.cindylgentry.com.

Hay House Titles of Related Interest

We hope you enjoyed this Hay House book. If you'd like to receive our online catalog featuring additional information on Hay House books and products, or if you'd like to find out more about the Hay Foundation, please contact:

Hay House, Inc., P.O. Box 5100, Carlsbad, CA 92018-5100
(760) 431-7695 or (800) 654-5126
(760) 431-6948 (fax) or (800) 650-5115 (fax)
www.hayhouse.com® • www.hayfoundation.org

———

Published in Australia by: Hay House Australia Pty. Ltd.,
18/36 Ralph St., Alexandria NSW 2015
Phone: 612-9669-4299 • *Fax:* 612-9669-4144
www.hayhouse.com.au

Published in the United Kingdom by: Hay House UK, Ltd.,
The Sixth Floor, Watson House, 54 Baker Street, London W1U 7BU
Phone: +44 (0)20 3927 7290 • *Fax:* +44 (0)20 3927 7291
www.hayhouse.co.uk

Published in India by: Hay House Publishers India,
Muskaan Complex, Plot No. 3, B-2, Vasant Kunj, New Delhi 110 070
Phone: 91-11-4176-1620 • *Fax:* 91-11-4176-1630
www.hayhouse.co.in

———

Access New Knowledge.
Anytime. Anywhere.

Learn and evolve at your own pace
with the world's leading experts.

www.hayhouseU.com